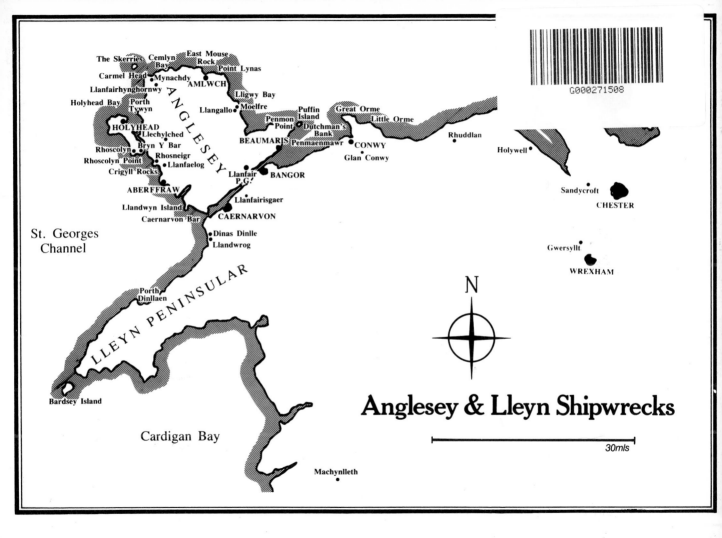

The Skerries
Cemlyn Bay
East Mouse Rock
Point Lynas
Carmel Head
Mynachdy
AMLWCH
Llanfairhynghornwy
Lligwy Bay
Holyhead Bay
Porth Tywyn
Moelfre
Llangallo
Puffin Island
Great Orme
Little Orme
HOLYHEAD
Llechylched
Penmon Point
Dutchman's Bank
Rhuddlan
Bryn Y Bar
BEAUMARIS
Rhoscolyn
Penmaenmawr
CONWY
Rhoscolyn Point
Rhosneirg
Glan Conwy
Holywell
Crigyll Rocks
Llanfaelog
Llanfair P.G.
BANGOR
Sandycroft
ABERFFRAW
Llanfairisgaer
CHESTER
Llandwyn Island
CAERNARVON
Gwersyllt
Caernarvon Bar
WREXHAM
Dinas Dinlle
Llandwrog

A N G L E S E Y

St. Georges Channel

Porth Dinllaen

LLEYN PENINSULAR

N

Bardsey Island

Cardigan Bay

Machynlleth

Anglesey & Lleyn Shipwrecks

30mls

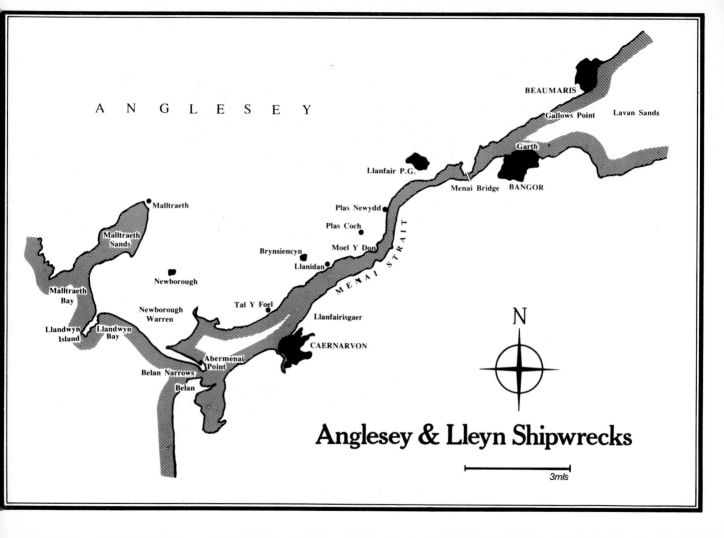

Anglesey & Lleyn Shipwrecks

3mls

ANGLESEY & LLEYN SHIPWRECKS

IAN SKIDMORE

CHRISTOPHER DAVIES

Published by
Christopher Davies (Publishers) Ltd.,
P.O. Box 403, Sketty,
Swansea, SA2 9BE.

Reprinted 1988

ISBN 0 7154 0704 X

*Set in 12 on 14 Baskerville and
Printed in Wales by
Dynevor Printing Company,
Rawlings Road, Llandybïe, Dyfed.*

By the same author:

ESCAPE FROM THE RISING SUN   Leo Cooper (1973)
WILDLIFE IN CUSTODY (with Ken Williams)   Cassel & Co. Ltd. (1977)
OWAIN GLYNDŴR, PRINCE OF WALES   Christopher Davies, Swansea (1978)
LIFEBOAT V.C.   David & Charles Ltd. (1979)

Acknowledgements

Capt. Geoffrey Butterworth MRIN
Ray Kipling, Asst. Press Officer RNLI
J. Clifford Jones, Asst. County Librarian
Mr and Mrs John Cave
My daughter Lynn May and my son-in-law Richard
Flt. Lt. R. Barrett, PRO RAF Valley
Mrs Dilys Parry
Bryn R. Parry the County Archivist and his staff at the Gwynedd Archive.
Inspector T. E. Williams, M.B.E., H. M. Coastguard (Retd.)
And to my wife Celia my special thanks for all her good work — not least her efforts
in compiling the index, translating Welsh documents and deciphering my crabbed
fist to produce the MS of this book. Also to that nameless host of newspaper
reporters who shivered on many a windswept beach collecting the material on
which some of the stories in this book are based.

For Bill Buxton, craftsman

Contents

List of Illustrations

The 'Rothsay Castle' disaster by M. P. Calvert engraved by J. Kirkwood showing her loss in 1831.

National Maritime Museum Archive.

Day-trip to Death

The *Rothsay Castle* had been one of the first steam driven vessels when she was launched in 1812. By 1831 she was, quite simply, a coffin ship. She was designed to ply up and down the River Clyde between Inverary and Glasgow. She was never intended as a sea-going vessel, her four-inch upper timbers were woefully inadequate for rough waters. She was six years over the age-limit the Royal Navy imposed on its own ships. Her single 50 h.p. engine was worn-out and incapable of driving her 200 tons through the steep seas of Liverpool Bay. She had only one lifeboat which would hold sixteen people but it had no oars and the only signal gun in case of distress was an ancient fowling piece.

The *Castle* had originally been bought by a Liverpool businessman, Thomas Watson, to run a packet service between Liverpool and Wexford. When, *en route* from the Clyde to the Wexford packet station, she had put in at Peel, Isle of Man, three of her crew of five, alarmed by her unseaworthiness, signed off and paid their own passage home. She was re-routed to Liverpool to hire extra hands but even the wretched wharf-rats who would sign on with any vessel for grog money refused to ship out in the *Castle*. When she put off from Liverpool for Beaumaris there were only two seamen aboard.

The sky was leaden and the Mersey, still restless five hours after the gale had dropped, went on buffeting the Pier Head. A band played jaunty music and few in the good-humoured crowd which bumped and jostled its way along the landing stage to the paddle steamer showed any apprehension at the prospect of a rough passage to Anglesey. The men wore coats over their blazers. Many sported naval caps with shiny peaks — in 1831 it was the height of fashion to copy the bluff sailor-king, William IV. And not even the appalling weather that August could snuff the brightness of the women's clothes, nor the glint in many an eye, shadowed by a straw boater, as its owner tried unsuccessfully to pretend she would resist any attempt at a shipboard flirtation.

They were a mixed crowd; the ribald and the genteel, the well-to-do and the threadbare worker blowing his savings on a day's jaunt, the only holiday he could afford. The Napoleonic Wars were over, the industrial prosperity they brought had been followed by trade recession and money was tight among the working classes. But for a time all cares had been left in the pages of newspapers that now littered the seats and decks of the horse buses that had brought them to the Liverpool dock. There was certainly no gloom among the twenty-six 'bloods' on their annual outing from the Grey Mare Hotel in Bury. They had even brought their own barmaid, a pert 23-year-old, Selina Lamb. Tom Entwistle, a cotton spinner and a bachelor, was sure of lively company on the boat.

For Margaret Walmsley the trip had a special significance. She was celebrating her engagement to a farmer named Fitton. The outing would mark the day in a way they would remember all their lives. It was a plan that was to have a macabre fulfilment. William Tarry was celebrating too, though in the restrained way befitting the considerable person he was. Steward to the enormously wealthy Lord Derby he had just taken the most important step in his life. The holiday in Anglesey for William, his wife and their four children, celebrated the leasing of a large farm on Lord Derby's Lancashire estate. A thoughtful man and, as he was to prove, totally devoted to his family, he had even brought a 17-year-old servant girl, Rachel Haworth, to relieve his wife of the burden of looking after the children.

The Tarrys were not the most consequential family on the vessel. Sailing was delayed for an hour so that the carriage of W. M. Foster, a society swell travelling

14

with his wife, her pet dog and a liveried footman, could be hauled aboard the steamer. The notion that he had delayed one hundred and fifty people for an hour (by his gold repeater) weighed lightly with Foster, a man with a town house in Cumberland Terrace, Regents Park, and 300 sovereigns jingling in his pocket.

There were, among the passengers, three well-to-do men from Rochdale: William Bottomley, George King and a colliery superintendent Ben Lees. From Liverpool James Lea and his brother-in-law travelled in the distinguished company of Member of Parliament George Canning's former secretary, de Sousa. There were all sorts of occupations represented on the boat. There was a Liverpool pilot, William Jones, returning to station at Point Lynas; Michael Griffiths, a seaman, was travelling to his home port in Bangor with his wife and child. There was a chemist from Chesterfield, a solicitor from Bradford, a Chorlton-cum-Hardy farmer, a Dublin priest and a Birmingham tea dealer.

And all the time these passengers were going aboard the ship's officers were 'drumming' up more by loud hailer. As a result they were dangerously over-crowded by the time the *Rothsay Castle* put to sea. But they were, at that time, just a crowd like other crowds all over the country that day. Crowds boarding trains to go to the seaside, crowds which would form later in the foyers of theatres, at circuses, in bars and boxing booths. There was no special mark on the people who queued good-humouredly and waited patiently for the smart, travelling coach to be lifted aboard the *Rothsay Castle*. Nothing to show that ninety-three people were only a day's voyage from death.

The tragedy which was to follow in twelve hours was more than partly due to the delay caused by loading the coach. By the time the paddle steamer cast off at 10 a.m. the tide had turned, slowing her down to such a degree that she reached the

15

dangerous Dutchman's Bank at the entrance to the Menai Straits at dead low water. By any standards, appalling seamanship.

The *Rothsay Castle's* captain was an ex-Royal Navy lieutenant called Atkinson. He had the sailor's rough affability. When the passengers boarded he walked among them chafing the pretty girls who thought him attentive and charming. 'Quite unexceptionable', one was to recall. It was a view they might have modified if they could have heard a conversation which at the moment of sailing was going on below decks.

Jones, the Liverpool pilot, had been invited for a drink to the steward's cabin. He was surprised to notice that his host was worried and his manner was abstracted as he poured out two hefty tots of rum.

'It's the captain,' the steward confessed. 'He doesn't expect to reach Beaumaris. This is going to be his last voyage.'

Did the captain appreciate the danger in putting to sea in the leaky tub he now commanded? If so, why did he take the risk? The answer might have been in the economic conditions of the day. In peacetime the Navy is whittled down and there are always more captains than there are ships to command. Perhaps it was the thought of all the other captains who would leap to take his place if he refused to obey his owner's sailing orders. Certainly he was a worried man. The *Castle* had scarcely cast off before he went down to his cabin and began to drink. Survivors later testified that two hours later their affable captain was drunk and no longer the 'quite unexceptionable' officer of the Pier Head.

The *Rothsay Castle* worked the Beaumaris service in tandem with the *Prince Llewellyn*. When the two ships passed at the entrance to the Mersey the *Llewellyn's* crew noticed with alarm that the *Castle* was far to the leeward of her safe course. There had been a north, north-west wind blowing strongly and Atkinson's vessel had been battling against a flood tide ever since she crossed the Mersey Bar. In such conditions, his 50 h.p. engine hopelessly underpowered, the *Rothsay Castle* should have been taken out to sea away from the dangerous lee shore. This seaward course, keeping north, north-west until daylight with a fair wind and a flood tide, would have carried him to Beaumaris. The passengers had been frightened by the pitching and rolling before they reached the Floating Light, an illuminated buoy only 15 miles out from Liverpool. To further alarm them they could hear Atkinson violently abusing his crew. The affability they had remarked in Liverpool had been dropped. What they were now seeing was the rough discipline of a time-serving Navy man.

Consternation grew, and the holiday spirit vanished completely. In the saloon the trippers sat at first in protective family groups. Then, as each sensed the family at the next table was equally apprehensive, the groups grew larger until the whole saloon was united in its fear.

Inevitably it was Mr Tarry who took command. He had years of experience in mediating between Derby and his tenants.

'I'll see the captain,' he offered. 'It's what everybody wants. I'll beg him to return to Liverpool.'

With another passenger to support him Mr Tarry went to the captain's cabin but the captain had been drinking steadily since they left port. His eyes were wild and angry, his voice thick and his tone sarcastic.

'I think there is a damn deal of fear aboard,' he told them contemptuously. 'And very little danger. If we were to turn back now with passengers it would never do: there would be very little profit.'

The second passenger, thoroughly frightened now, tried to urge the captain to change his mind but he was shouted down by the angry, drunken mariner.

'I'm not one of those that turn back. If you knew me you would not ask that! We will be in Beaumaris by 7 p.m.'

In the event it was long after dark before the terrified passengers, peering white-faced through the saloon windows, saw the bulk of the Little Orme. Had they known it, this was their last chance. Between the two Ormes there is a four fathoms anchorage. Atkinson might have anchored there, keeping up enough steam to hold the *Rothsay Castle* off the shore for long enough to land the women and children in the ship's boat. Even without oars they would stand a better chance of reaching safety than they did in the *Castle* and the men might have lashed casks, ladders and planking into rafts. But the captain was determined to complete the passage.

It took four hours for the *Rothsay Castle,* by this time leaking badly, to reach the Great Orme at the far end of Llandudno. By 11 p.m., a seaman was to testify, neither the skipper nor the mate was sober and water was pouring through the steamer's seams. The bilge pumps were choked, the coal in the holds was totally submerged and the cabins were awash. It was only a matter of time before wet coals damped out the fire.

In the engine room stoker Will Jones had switched on the pumps at 10 p.m. but they were useless against the sea which was pouring through the shaft on the paddle wheels.

The distant lights of Conway offered a faint hope to the passengers and once again they stormed the captain's cabin.

'I implore you to put in at Conway,' a passenger begged. The captain shook the brandy fumes out of his head. There was no trace of the naval bully boy in his voice now.

'God keep me from attempting it,' he replied. 'It would be instant destruction.'

The ship arrived at the mouth of the Menai Straits at midnight with the tide running against her and the head of steam so low that the *Castle* could not keep on course. Helplessly they drifted towards the Dutchman's Bank, the long spit of sand which has been the graveyard of many ships.

Yet there was still a chance of rescue. Less than half a mile away at Penmon Point there was a pilot station. A single rocket fired, a light shown, and a rescue boat could have been on the scene within ten minutes. There were twenty vessels lying off Bangor which could have taken all the passengers at the flash of a lantern. Yet, incredibly, the *Rothsay Castle* carried no lantern.

'For God's sake fire a gun,' Robert Whittaker, a passenger, begged.

'There is not one aboard,' the captain told him. 'Only a fowling piece.'

By now the panic was spreading from the passengers to the crew. William Jones climbed into the rigging shouting: 'We are all lost.' The helmsman, William Hughes, refused to obey the captain's order to put the helm to starboard, putting it instead to port, wrestling with the mate who tried to remove him.

The passengers, ignoring the captain, rang the ship's bell with such force that the clapper disintegrated. They beat it with sticks and lumps of coal. Its peals were heard in Beaumaris — but because there was no light there was no way of telling the position of the ship.

Inevitably the *Rothsay Castle* struck the Dutchman's Bank.

'It's only sand,' the captain reassured the passengers. 'She will soon float off.' And he ordered them to run aft to lighten the prow. Scrambling and slipping over the soaking deck the passengers, some crying in their fright, did as they were bid. But no sooner had they reached the stern than the captain made them run forward. The jib sail was run up in the hope of bringing the *Castle's* head to the south but it was too late. The *Rothsay Castle* was stuck fast.

The captain tried to reassure the passengers; although he knew better than

19

anyone how desperate their plight was.

'There is no danger. The packet is afloat and doing well,' he told them. But the pilot clinging to the rigging knew better. Convinced he was bout to die, Jones counted the number of times the *Castle* struck the sandbank before it came to rest. He had reached 50 before he heard the captain give the order to go astern.

Passengers were hurled into the sea with every impact. It is estimated that fifty lost their lives and perhaps they were the luckiest. For they missed the sights which were to stay with the survivors for the rest of their lives. One recalled:

'The females, in particular, uttered the most piercing shrieks: some locked themselves in each others arms, while others, losing all self command, tore their caps and bonnets in the wildness of their despair. The women and children collected in a knot together and kept embracing each other, uttering all the time the most dismal lamentations. When tired with crying they leaned against each other with their heads reclined, like inanimate bodies.'

In their blind panic no one apparently realised that under the *Rothsay Castle's* bows were stretches of sand where the bottom was drying out. They could have waited there in safety until they were rescued.

Henry Hammond, a ship's carpenter, had been trying to comfort the *Castle* carpenter's wife and child. He had wrapped his arms round them and forced his way to the single ship's boat. He had just lifted them in when the *Castle* struck for the final time but as he was climbing aboard himself the mate ran up and ordered them out.

'It's no use,' he told Hammond, 'no boat could live in this weather.'

They had barely clambered out onto the deck before a huge wave swamped the small boat and tipped it upside-down into the sea. It was washed up the next day, a total wreck, below Beaumaris.

20

The *Castle* itself now began to break up. The two stays which supported the funnel snapped. A deck hand immediately repaired them but they snapped again and the stack came crashing down, bringing the mast with it, crushing the steward and his wife who had lashed themselves to it and finally falling on a group of passengers on the starboard side of the deck.

Hammond meanwhile had reunited the ship's carpenter with his wife and child but as he wrapped his cloak round the wife's soaked and shivering body another tremendous wave hit the deck washing her and eleven other passengers overboard. The captain fell as he struggled across the deck. The mate, bending to help him, slipped and both were washed overboard to their deaths.

Jones, the pilot, was more fortunate. A local man, he knew that they must be near the shore. Tying himself to a barrel and holding a discarded umbrella he jumped into the sea. When he hit the water he unfurled the brolly, held it out in front of him and, using it as a sail, reached the shore and was saved.

Miss Mary Whittaker had been dragged onto a makeshift raft by a male passenger and his six companions. Without oars every wave carried them farther from the land. A whispered argument broke out among her deliverers who kept looking at her and waving angrily. At length one of them broke away and slithered across to her side. She saw he was blushing.

'What is it?' she asked. It was some seconds before he plucked up the courage to tell her.

'We need your skirt for a sail otherwise we will be swept out to sea.'

Astonishingly the argument among the seven men had been over the propriety of asking Miss Whittaker to take off her skirt.

She not only took off the skirt, she gave them her garters as well! Holding the skirt before them, with Miss Whittaker in her bloomers, waving her handkerchief as a distress signal, it was not long before they were saved.

Mr Tarry had behaved with great calmness throughout the nightmare passage. When the *Rothsay Castle* first hit bad weather he locked his family and their servant in their cabin whilst he repeatedly asked what hope there was. Told there was none, but that he might save himself, he shook his head.

'I must return to my cabin to die with them,' he said. 'I brought my family out and to return without them would be worse than death.'

They were not to die together. His youngest daughter, a pretty 10-year-old, ran out of the cabin. Wandering along the quarter deck calling broken-heartedly for help she was knocked off her feet by a wave which dashed her against the gunwales. Then, floating back in its ebb, she was smashed against the gunwales of the opposite side of the boat. A survivor, Lawrence Duck, remembered:

'She was bruised and bleeding and half choked with sea water but I could hear her crying over and over again "Oh won't you come to me Mamma. Oh Father . . .".' She was the only one of the family to be saved.

Similar family tragedies were being enacted all over the ship. James Broadhurst, a Sheffield man, lost two daughters. He had struggled across the deck with his children in his arms until he found a place on the galley roof where he thought they would be safe. He lifted them up in turn but as he moved to join them a falling spar knocked him into the sea. Ironically he survived but both girls were lost.

Mr Duck had also made his way to the deck galley dragging his exhausted wife with him. He lifted her up next to the Broadhurst children and was just scrambling up to join her when the wave struck — washing the three to their deaths.

A Manchester man, Henry Wilson, was saved but his wife drowned. As she was washed away he could hear her calling, 'Save yourself, Henry! Save yourself! Save yourself for the sake of the children!'

James Martin, a Liverpool shoemaker, and his friend Mark Metcalfe, a leather cutter, were on their knees praying when the ship struck. Scrambling to their feet they pushed their way through the crowd of frightened passengers to a plank which was stretched between the paddle-box out of reach of even the highest of the waves which were crashing over the deck.

Martin said afterwards: 'The waves were continually dashing over us with great impetuosity, sweeping away passengers at every stroke.'

After a while the waves dropped, and in the comparative quiet which followed, Martin looked about him for his friend Metcalfe.

He said: 'I found him still at his post, clinging to the iron. I asked him if he had a firm grip. He answered "Yes, but I am nearly exhausted". At this period, all the passengers who previously held on to the paddle iron under the plank had disappeared, from the violence of the breakers, except my friend Metcalfe and another person. A short time only had elapsed and I saw him carried away by a dreadful wave exclaiming: "James, I'm afraid it's all over . . .".'

A moment later the plank on which Martin and about twenty other passengers were crouched gave way hurling them into the breakers.

His head singing, his lungs bursting and the salt burning his eyes, Martin sank deep into the sea under the *Rothsay Castle*. Struggling wildly on the edge of hysteria he found himself being carried to the surface. By the greatest good fortune he surfaced at the side of the identical plank from which he had fallen into the sea and, grabbing it, he survived.

A Londoner named Coxhead had another remarkable escape. He was washed overboard no less than four times but each time he managed to scramble back on board.

The Bury chemist, Nuttall, managed to stay on the *Castle* until 1.30 a.m. when she broke up. He remembered the last moments vividly:

'The shrieks of anguish and despair were deafening as terrific waves swept over the decks. I was thrown into the sea encumbered by my great coat and a small boy who took refuge on my back. I must have drowned had not providence thrown a rope my way. I seized it and was drawn to a part of the wheelhouse that adhered to the wheel.'

In all there were only 23 survivors and their plight won them great sympathy from the Beaumaris people. The local M.P., Richard Bulkely Williams Bulkely, raised funds for them and they and the relatives of the dead found a welcome in homes all over the town.

Watson, the owner, received a very rough reception when he arrived the next day. He seemed unmoved. He charged relatives £5 a corpse for taking the dead back to Liverpool in the *Llewellyn* and he is said to have laughed immoderately when a survivor told him how the captain had behaved.

Criticised at the fund raising meeting — which, incredibly, he attended — he rose to his feet and shouted: 'You must not think this is the only place my ships could go to.'

Sir Richard told the meeting: 'I hope to be able to keep my temper within bounds and restrain as much as possible the indignation I feel and which I have no doubt is felt by every man in this room at the conduct of Mr Watson since the melancholy catastrophe which has plunged so many families into grief and despair . . . I shall only say, however, that the *Rothsay Castle* was known and acknowledged by the people of this place and of Liverpool to have been an unsound vessel.'

When he sat down a Liverpool alderman, John Wright, rose to add his condemnation of Watson.

'I cannot express my indignation in too forcible terms at the apathy and want of common feeling exhibited by him on this melancholy occasion.'

Sir Richard returned to the attack at the inquest on one of the dead. He was foreman of the Jury and it is his signature which appears at the end of a rider which they added to the verdict of death by drowning.

It read: 'From the evidence brought before them, the jury at this inquest cannot separate without expressing their firm conviction that had the *Rothsay Castle* been a seaworthy vessel and properly manned, this awful calamity might have been averted. They, therefore, cannot disguise their indignation at the conduct of those who could place such a vessel on this station and under the charge of a captain and a mate who have been proved by the evidence brought before them to have been in a state of intoxication.'

Bodies were being washed ashore for miles up the coast. Mrs Tarry is buried on the Great Orme, her two-year-old son John in Glanconwy churchyard. One man is buried in Formby while his wife is one of the many buried in Beaumaris churchyard.

The *Rothsay Castle* disaster lingered in the memory of nervous passengers for many years. In 1842 a steamer from Beaumaris was passing Puffin Island when the news spread among the passengers that water was shipping in and pouring on the coals in the engine room. They insisted on pulling back and, though the crew spent the whole day putting matters right, few of the passengers could be coaxed back on board. They preferred to return to Liverpool by night coach. This was hardly less hazardous as a report in a 19th century copy of the *North Wales Chronicle* indicates. It tells the story of a Mr W. Davies of Holywell who fell off the Holyhead coach a few seconds after it left the White Lion Inn, St Asaph. The account continues:

'Strangely enough neither passengers, guard nor coachman took the slightest notice of the unfortunate man who was discovered quite by chance by a lady out

HM Coastguard Operations Room Aberdaron, overlooking Bardsey Sound.   A Neilson Photograph.

26

walking. He died in agony two days later.'

It did not matter. Passengers were still wary of the steamers. A leader in the same issue pointed out:

'Parties from Manchester especially, intending to visit the Welsh Coast have been deterred from venturing in consequence of the rumoured insecurity of some of the steamers and changed their destination for the Isle of Man. This fact speaks volumes. It is not without cause that people apprehend such another calamity as the wreck of the *Rothsay Castle*.'

There have been fifty recorded wrecks between Puffin Island and Beaumaris, many of them on the Dutchman's Bank, but few have been wrecked deliberately. This distinction goes to the *MV Gleneden* on January 28th, 1940.

The *Gleneden*, a cargo ship out of Glasgow carrying a cargo of iron vital to the war effort, was torpedoed in a south-easterly gale off Bardsey Island. Although she was badly holed her pumps were holding their own against the seas which were pouring through the ship's side and the skipper decided to make a run for the nearest port, Holyhead. As they limped through heavy seas the force of the water enlarged the holes the torpedo had made but, incredibly, the *Gleneden* kept afloat and the skipper decided to make a final run for the port of Liverpool. Half-way between Holyhead and Point Lynas the overworked pumps began to fail and a desperate race began to find somewhere to beach the *Gleneden* so that at least the cargo could be salvaged. The Dutchman's Bank, the graveyard for hundreds of seamen, was chosen. Lifeboats at Moelfre and Beaumaris were launched to go to her assistance as the *Gleneden* steamed down the flank of Anglesey.

Wartime services were a nightmare to lifeboat crews. There were no shore lights to guide them and lighthouses operated on half power. Lights like Penmon which in peacetime was shown every minute had their frequency reduced to ten minute intervals. If the cox missed the light it was another twenty minutes before he saw it again. The busy shipping lanes round the island were crowded with convoys and flotillas of mine-sweepers. None showed lights and the lifeboatmen put to sea knowing that any minute their boat might be run down under the bows of a merchantman. Navigation was by dead reckoning and for John Matthews, coxswain of the Moelfre lifeboat, the passage to the Dutchman's Bank was especially difficult. There were no echo-sounders on the lifeboat and in the early days of the war there was not even radio. But by sheer seamanship Matthews managed to skirt the Penmon rocks and the shoaling water round Puffin Island to come up on the stern of the *Gleneden* which by this time had buried her bows firmly into the wet sand.

Aware all the time of the danger of running his own craft aground Matthews came round her stern and bumped up the side of the iron hull which towered above him to the humping ladder amidships. One by one, the crew of 45 lascars came tumbling down into the lifeboat until she was down to her gunwales and dangerously overcrowded. Filled with shivering, frightened men, buffeted by the heavy seas and sailing blind, the lifeboat somehow got to Beaumaris Pier where a fleet of field ambulances was waiting.

No sooner was the last man ashore than Matthews raced back to the *Gleneden* where the skipper and his fifteen white officers were waiting.

By this time the *Gleneden* was yawing under the punishment she had taken from the sea and it could only be a matter of moments before she broke up.

Matthews sent his second cox, Dick Evans, up the ladder to warn the officers that if they did not leave at once there would be no hope of saving them. Evans had barely climbed up the swaying rope-ladder to the deck before, with an explosion that tore the night apart, the ship's back broke. Even so, the skipper refused to leave the deck

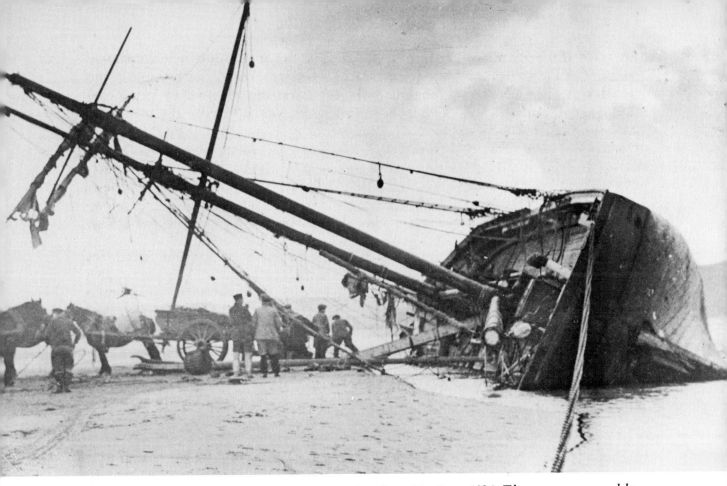

The wreck of the schooner 'Flying Foam' at Llanidloes 21st June 1936. The crew were saved by Beaumaris lifeboat. She was carrying a cargo of coal.

Gwynedd Archives Service.

Outward bound from Liverpool in 1898, the 'SS Dahomey' encountered thick fog off Holyhead and ran aground at Porth Namarch.

until the last of his officers was on the ladder. They were hardly underweight before the *Gleneden* began to break up.

The sixty men of the *Gleneden* were lucky. Year after year the Dutchman's Bank and the Lavan sands claimed vessels and more often than not the lives of their sailors. The names read like a roll-call of shipping.

In 1832 the sloop *Atlas.*

In 1833 the brig *Jane and Ann,* two days later the *St George* and the *Aukland,* three days later a schooner, the next day three more vessels.

In 1837 the *Britannia.*

In 1844 the *Elinor.*

The *Royal Charter* gale in 1859 brought more disasters. The *Messenger,* out of Caernarvon, was wrecked just beyond Beaumaris lifeboat station. The year after the *Gleneden* broke up *HMS St Olave,* a 468-ton tug, was holed on a rock near Puffin Island.

In December 1945 the MV *River Loyne* vanished after leaving Penmaenmawr with a cargo of stone. Some days later the tip of her mast was seen above the waves a mile off Puffin Island but her crew were never found. Even experienced seamen can be caught in the treacherous waters at the mouth of the Straits. Racing for shelter with two other Conway trawlers, the *Glenmaye* struck a submerged rock and her crew had to swim for Puffin Island.

Lord Langford of Bodrhyddan Hall, Rhuddlan, is no stranger to the sea. When Singapore fell his lordship, at that time a young Gunner major, escaped and with a group of fellow officers sailed a patched and leaking Malay parhau 1,500 miles across the Bay of Bengal from Sumatra to Ceylon. On August 19th, 1970, while out boating with his sons and friends, his borrowed cabin cruiser, the *Wendy Sue,* sank at her moorings leaving them stranded on Puffin Island. Waiting to be rescued by the Beaumaris lifeboat was not a pleasant experience. The party discovered that the island was alive with rats which had swum there from earlier wrecks and bred in their thousands.

Wreck of white diamond steamer 'Missouri' during worst snow storm ever experienced on Anglesey, March 1, 1886.

The Bloody Shore

The Legions had marched from Chester and, to the Celtic tribesmen who watched them from their hiding place in the woods, the columns of metal men must have looked like a monstrous machine thundering behind a god on a white horse. Detachments of auxiliary cavalry had ridden ahead of the general and his staff, probing, ever vigilant. Behind, the main body rode and behind them came the infantry in numbers beyond counting.

To the tribesmen it was the infantryman who inspired the greatest awe. In another country it had been said of the Roman soldier that he looked as though his weapons were permanently attached to him. They were the greatest fighting machine in the Ancient World.

The 60-mile march from Chester to Anglesey took three days and the pace of these supermen never varied whether they marched along the even military roads, over mountain scree or across boggy moorland. Their heavy leather sandals, studded with hobnails, were indifferent to cobbled roads, shifting pebbles and springy turf alike. Their heavy wooden shields slung, they ported their two javelins lightly and a dagger and a stabbing sword swung at every waist.

Behind the infantry the siege train rumbled. Teams of horses dragged *ballistae*, flame throwers on rough wooden platforms, which could fling a 12-ft flaming dart 2,000 feet or more; *onagers* to hurl boulders or bags of small rocks which could decimate an enemy line. Besides the crossbows, the onagers and the ballistae, the train carried equipment not usually seen in a Roman train. The long flat-bottomed boats had been the general's inspiration. Normally the legions made their water crossings by ingenious bridgeworks laid and lashed on a vertebra of small boats. But the water they were marching to cross was too swift and dangerous for such a bridge. Its currents and whirlpools would have plucked at a bridge of boats like harp strings until they had snapped and hurled the legions to their deaths: for the purpose of the legions on this march was a seaborne invasion across the Menai Straits to Anglesey, the Mother Island, and the last stronghold in Roman occupied Britain of the Druids and their followers.

In A.D. 61 the Druids on Anglesey had held out against the Romans for one hundred years and to the general, Seutonius Paulinus, the Military Governor of Britain, it was unthinkable that this affront to his military reputation should continue. He anticipated little trouble. The men of the 14th and 20th Legions who marched behind him were most of them veterans of many campaigns. With their superiority of arms and the sophisticated battlefield techniques they had practised all over Europe they outclassed the Druids' force of lightly armed tribesmen, undisciplined men in skins with only small targes for protection. At last the threat the Druids posed to the Roman occupation was coming to an end. The refugees who had flocked to the sanctuary of the Mother Island would learn that nowhere were they beyond the reach of Rome. Most important of all, the copper mountain of Parys which had provided the metal for British weapons would pass into Roman hands.

The legions probably made their base camp on the mainland shore below Llanfairisgaer (Mary's Church below the camp) and the preparations for the invasion began. The flat-bottomed boats were carried down to the water's edge and the cavalry were ordered to swim their horses across. That in itself was daunting even for seasoned soldiers but it was the sight on the far shore which started the mutterings in the Imperial army.

Ranged along the high ground above the shore were thousands of tribesmen. In the van of this army robed Druids, their staffs raised to heaven, invoked dark gods and poured imprecations on the Romans. Through the ranks danced wild-haired women, their naked bodies painted in the colours of nightmare, waving blazing torches, warming the blood lust of the warriors.

The Romans were riveted with terror. They stood numbed, staring at the awful visions across the Straits that seemed like the Furies of their own hagiology.

It was unthinkable to Seutonius, a professional soldier, that a Roman army could behave in this way. A man from a class which had been trained for centuries to ignore fear, he had no comprehension of the terror to which they had succumbed. But it required all his eloquence to chase out the fear that gripped them. He chided them for their cowardice and no doubt reminded them that their fate when they returned in disgrace to Rome would be far worse than anything that might happen to them on Anglesey. He began to win individual soldiers round and as the braver ones in turn took up his taunts every man in the legions began to feel his courage return and at last the boats were launched.

Not all those clumsy barges made the crossing; and today the bones of Roman soldiers rest in the mud at the bottom of the Straits side by side with the mariners of nineteen centuries. But enough succeeded for a landing in force to be made and the slaughter began. Under the goad of the shame at their earlier cowardice — and perhaps to find favour in their general's eye — the legions stabbed and killed with a fury which was unusual for them. And there is little doubt that they were spurred on by the general. Seutonius Paulinus might have been a brilliant soldier — but even by the standards of Imperial Rome he was a cruel man. Tacitus said of him:

'He proceeded always against the vanquished, even after they had surrendered, with excessive rigour. Justice under his administration had frequently the air of personal injury. Indeed, his public proceedings and his private passions became so mixed that he was recalled to Rome.'

There is no telling when the slaughter would have ended, nor how many Druids and their followers were thrown alive into the blazing pyres of their Holy Oak graves. Fortunately Seutonius had barely begun to garrison the island before he and his legions were recalled to quell the revolt led by Boadicea. The whole province of Britain was up in arms and Anglesey was spared. Another 15 years passed before Anglesey once again suffered an invasion by sea.

Agricola was a very different stamp of soldier from Seutonius Paulinus. Every bit as brave, he was a much more meticulous staff officer. He studied the terrain before he launched his invasion. Eschewing mass frontal attack he used auxiliary cavalry trained to swim by their horses and brought them in secretly across the Lavan Sands. But it is Seutonius Paulinus the land remembers. The Bloody Shore stretches from Moel-y-Don to Tal-y-Foel and the names of hillocks and fields and houses recall the slaughter of the first seaborne invasion. Below Moel-y-Don is Bryn-y-Beddau (the hill of graves) where the British buried their dead. Further down is the first of several houses called Plas Coch (the Red Mansion). Above the ruined church of Llanidan are two fields still named on ordnance maps as the Field of Bitter Lamentation and the Field of the Long Battle.

One thousand years later the Menai Straits were once again the scene of a seaborne invasion. In 1157 the forerunner of the British Navy suffered its first defeat off Anglesey when Henry II sent a combined English, Irish and Danish fleet to attack the island.

The fleet sailed from Rhuddlan under the command of a Welsh traitor prince, Madoc ap Meredith, and anchored off the island. Soldiers were put ashore where they despoiled two churches, raping and ravaging, before they returned to their ships. A contemporary chronicler, Giraldus, Gerald of Wales, reported the sequel:

'As they returned to their ships, all the strength of the Isle set upon them and killed them all so that none of those that robbed within the Isle brought tidings of how they sped. Then the shipmen seeing that, liked not their lodgings, but weighed up anchors and went away to Chester.'

Although only 250 yards across at their widest, the Menai Straits have claimed many lives, mainly from the ferry services established by Edward I in the 13th century. The earliest of these was at Bishop's Crossing between Gallows Point below Beaumaris and Cadnant Creek on the mainland. This ferry survived until 1850 when, like the Old Horse Ferry at Menai Bridge, it was made obsolete by Telford's iron suspension bridge. A tower of this bridge stands on Pig Island where, in the centuries before the ferries ran, livestock for market on the mainland were brought to rest in their swim across the Straits.

On October 6th, 1710, the Moel-y-Don ferry sank but happily the occupants, 15 men and 10 horses, were saved. Less fortunate were passengers on the Tal-y-Foel ferry 13 years later. This crossing had been established to carry stones from the island quarries for the walls of Caernarvon Castle in 1283. The first recorded passenger service was in 1425 and the first recorded disaster was on April 13th, 1723, when 30 people drowned. There were only two survivors, one of them a boy who grabbed the tail of a horse which pulled him to the shore. Early disasters were attributed to various causes, some of them supernatural. The cause of one was said to be that the boat had been built from wood stolen from Llanidan Church. This ruined church below the village of Brynsiencyn was a place of powerful magic. It is said to contain a stone in the shape of a human thigh bone which if it is removed will find its own way back to the church. A man who stole it stuffed it in his waistband. The next day, the story runs, the skin where it rested was horribly burned. Hugh the Fat, the Earl of Chester, is said to have wrapped the stone in chains and thrown it into the Straits. The next morning it was back in the church.

There must have been many occasions when passengers on the Abermenai ferry wished they shared the secret of the stone's power. It is a very short passage from the tip of Newborough Warren — where the ruins of the ferry house can still be seen — to Caernarvon. Yet there have been three ferry disasters on that passage involving the loss of 159 lives.

In the absence of a miracle stone it was just as well to be called Hugh Williams, as a curious footnote in a parish register of 1820 suggests. Written on the corner of the register is this note:

'Remarkable coincidence. In the year 1785 one of the Abermenai ferry-boats in returning from a fair at Caernarvon was lost, when all perished except one man a native of Anglesey Hugh Williams, Tynllwyden, Gent.

'On Saturday the 5th August 1820 another boat belonging to a new ferry adjacent to Caernavon being overloaded unfortunately sank when all perished except one man, a native of Anglesey whose name was Hugh Williams, Bodonwyn Isa.'

At the foot of the page is written in another hand:

'On Saturday being the tenth day of December 1664 the ferry boat at Abermenai missing whereby eightie poor souls and upwards lost their lives; one man saved named Hugh Williams. In Dec. 1785 in number perished 56, August 5th 1820 in number perished 23.'

The disaster in 1664 is said to have been caused by a dispute over the penny fare. The ferry, crowded with passengers returning from Caernarvon market, had crossed the Straits and reached the shore of Abermenai. A passenger insisted that he had already paid his fare, the ferryman was equally insistent that he had not. A row broke out which became so violent that neither the ferryman nor his passengers, no doubt engrossed by the argument, noticed that the ferry-boat was drifting. In a little time it had reached the narrow neck of water between the ferry station and Fort

Belan where it capsized in the rush of the tide. It was this sinking that superstitious islanders attributed to the use of wood stolen from Llanidan.

December 5th, 1785, was Fair Day in Caernarvon and the passengers for the short trip back to Anglesey may have been reluctant to leave the cheerful warmth of the pothouses for the icy, bone-chewing winds they would meet on the passage to Abermenai.

Whatever the reason, the ferry did not cast off until 4 p.m. that day, less than an hour from low water when the Straits, with their exposed sandbanks, are at their most hazardous. But it was by all accounts a cheery crowd which at last piled into the open boat, huddling together in the thwarts for warmth, perhaps singing carols.

As the boat with 54 people aboard moved out of the harbour it was raked by a strong south-easterly which sent its cold wet fingers burrowing into the passengers' travelling cloaks. So concerned were they to wrap themselves even more tightly in their clothes that no one noticed until they struck the sandbank that the wind had blown them out of the safe deep water channel.

Not even this alarming occurrence seems to have dampened their festive spirit. Still laughing and joking, full of excitement of the fair and possibly pot-house gin, the passengers scrambled onto the bank to push the ferry-boat into deep water. But the wind was too strong for them. The boat was torn from their hands, a wave under its keel lifted and capsized it and, before the terrified gaze of the passengers, it filled with water and sank.

The singing died to be replaced by cries for help but even then there seemed no cause for panic. The cries had carried to the mainland and it was not long before one after another a small flotilla of rowing boats put off from the shore.

Spirits revived at the sight and the shivering group on the bank waved their thanks, lifting first one wet foot and then the other out of the cold, wet sand into which they were sinking. Perhaps only the crew of the ferry-boat realised the danger they were in. They must have known that the bank shelved so gradually that none of the boats would be able to get near enough to the stranded parties to lift them to safety. One by one the rescue boats touched bottom and veered off. Unbelievingly, crying piteously, the trapped fifty-four watched as their rescuers made for the safety of the Caernarvon harbour.

None of the stranded passengers had a chance it seemed. The tide in the Straits rushed in like an express train and those must have been dreadful hours as they waited for high tide and the roar of rushing water in the darkness that would signal the end. At last it came and, one by one, as they scrambled desperately onto the highest spit of sand, the water lifted victims from their feet and sent them spinning, sodden bundles of clothes and flailing limbs, to their deaths.

Only Hugh Williams of Ty'n Llwyden — the house still stands overlooking the bay at Aberffraw — was spared. The tide smashed the ferry-boat to pieces against a submerged rock and as the mast bobbed to the surface Williams grabbed it. After two hours in the bitterly cold water he was washed ashore below the farm house at Tal-y-Foel.

Surprisingly, with such hazardous waters on their doorsteps, it was not until the 19th century that men began to think of improving rescue techniques. Not all the methods were conventional.

In 1867 the citizens of Bangor were startled to read in their weekly paper that John Rees of Machynlleth intended to walk on the water 'without losing his equilibrium'. More, 'he would besides go through several other rather extra-ordinary manoeuvres'.

Thousands gathered on the hillside of Garth outside the town to watch the performance and when Mr Rees appeared in a stiff oilskin suit the applause was deafening. When subsequently he sat down in the shallows and, taking two small oars from a pocket, rowed himself in a sitting position across the Straits to the Anglesey shore the cheers made the windows rattle half a mile away. But Mr Rees had not done with his audience. He made the return journey lounging nonchalently.on the waves and for an encore walked on the water for several yards before he touched bottom and waded, triumphantly, ashore.

Raising his hands and immediately commanding silence Mr Rees addressed the crowd:

'The apparatus of which I am the patenter and inventor,' he told them, 'consists of an air and waterproof dress which envelops the whole person without impeding the limbs. It contains eleven air and waterproof compartments, each completely independent of the other and under the perfect control of the occupant. When partially inflated it places the wearer in a perpendicular position which attitude can be easily maintained in the roughest sea in wildest storm. When fully inflated — a proceeding only recommended when the storm has abated — it permits the assumption of a sitting position in which the individual may, with the aid of accompanying paddles or even his own hands, propel himself in any direction at the rate of two to three miles an hour with perfect safety.'

In addition to the safety the comfort of the individual was considered. This remarkable suit contained sufficient compartments for several days' provisions. Nor did Mr Rees rest with saving the lives of individual mariners. He also patented a pneumatic apparatus which would cover an entire ship. His demonstration with a model which kept afloat though freighted with twice the proper cargo and holed in eight places was a complete success.

No doubt there were sceptics amongst the crowd and it is sadly true that after this single magnificent entry — in a sitting position — into the world's stage nothing more is traceable of Mr Rees. But it is difficult to watch the dinghy sailors who sail the Straits in their hundreds putting on their life-jackets without raising a spiritual hat to the pioneering genius of the man who walked on water.

Mr Rees's patented life-saving suit came 34 years too late for the wooden paddle steamer, *Monk,* which set out on January 6th, 1843, from Porth Dinllaen bound for Liverpool with a cargo of livestock.

By that time a lifeboat station had been established on Llandwyn Island but as luck would have it the Llandwyn pilots who manned the lifeboat had chosen that day to take her to Caernarvon and beached at Abermenai on the return passage.

The ramshackle *Monk* was a leaking tub in the most favourable seas. Weighed down as she was when she put to sea in a half gale at 2 p.m. that day with 140 pigs, 600 lbs of Welsh butter, 18 farmers and her crew of eight she was soon awash. Heavily overloaded and consequently low in the water, leaking badly and dangerously underpowered, it took two and a half hours for the *Monk* to reach the black buoy at the entrance to Caernarvon harbour. By that time the wind from the West-North-West was blowing a near hurricane yet, unaccountably, her master, Captain Hughes, a perverse and wilful man, decided against the safer but longer route round Anglesey. Instead, though he had no pilot aboard, he ordered a course through the Straits.

Hugh Jones, the *Monk*'s engineer was appalled. The ramshackle ship was already shipping water at a faster rate than the pumps could get rid of it. He begged the captain to make for port but it was already too late. At 5 p.m. the chain of the ship's wheel broke and within half an hour the *Monk* was aground on a sandbank being pounded by waves which, according to eye-witnesses, were thirty feet high.

The disaster might have been avoided if the *Monk* had carried an experienced pilot. It still lacked two hours to low water when they ran aground but the situation of those aboard was soon desperate.

Despite the intimidating waves which were breaking over the ship's side, Hugh Jones and another seaman, Owen Williams from Birmingham, decided to take their chance in the ship's boat. Two farmers, Thomas Davies and Thomas Jones, agreed to go with them. It was a brave decision. A contemporary wrote after the disaster:

'No one unacquainted with the locality can form any idea of the terrific surf that runs on these banks during West-North-West gales. Some affirm that they curl over at a height of not much less than thirty feet.'

In the event the boat's crew survived but of the twenty men they left behind only two were alive when dawn broke the next morning.

At midnight the *Monk's* back had broken under the breakers and her stern was smashed to pieces. Sixteen men were swept to their deaths in an instant. The other four, including Captain Hughes, escaped by clinging to the forrard rigging. Another man died in the night and by 7 p.m. the captain decided that he could hold on no longer.

'I'm going to try swimming,' he shouted and before anyone could stop him he had leapt into the surf. It was the last wrong decision he ever made. He drowned almost at once and days later his body was found on the shore surrounded by the carcasses of dead pigs.

To the two men who remained, slumped and barely conscious in the rigging, it must have seemed that their own deaths were only moments away. In fact deliverance was at hand. Luckily for them Captain John Jones of Bodiowerth, Newborough, rode his pony along the foreshore every morning. He saw the two survivors clinging to the rigging and galloped to Abermenai where the Llandwyn boat was beached to raise the alarm. Manhandling the lifeboat down to the water's edge and launching her into the breakers, the crew, with Captain Jones shouting encouragement in the stern, snatched the freezing survivors from their perch on the rigging. They were just in time. A wave hit the foredeck just as they were pulling away from the *Monk* and the rigging collapsed in a cloud of spume.

The lifeboat crew were to get little thanks for their efforts. At the inquest on one of the drowned men a survivor, Thomas Jones of Tair Dwr, made the first accusation against the men who had risked their own lives to save him. He told the Coroner, H. Hunter Hughes:

'Had the Llandwyn lifeboat been on its proper station all those aboard would have been saved.'

In a rider to his verdict Mr Hughes expressed his own great dissatisfaction at the absence of the boat and a wish that the matter would be investigated in the proper quarters.

The stage was set for a witch-hunt.

Thirty experts attended the Board of Inquiry at Caernarvon into the conduct of the lifeboatmen. Its brief was to discover if more lives would have been saved had the lifeboat been on station.

Once again Captain Jones came galloping to the rescue. Called as a witness he was quite emphatic. He told the Board:

'It was by the most merciful interposition of God that the boat happened to be at Abermenai and was thus enabled to save those who survived. Had the boat been on its station at Llandwyn this could not have been effected.'

Only slightly less impassioned but equally telling was the evidence of the Caernarvon Harbour Surveyor, Robert Roberts. Agreeing that it was in theory easier to reach the wreck from Llandwyn than Abermenai, he added:

'Under the circumstances of the darkness of the night no boat whatever could

Wreck of 'H.M.S. Conway' at Menai Bridge.

Henry Parry Collection, Gwynedd Archives Service.

have ventured to thread a narrow channel in the dark with a frightful surf tumbling all round. No mortal man in his senses would have thought of such a thing.'

The conflict of evidence which followed is evident in the Board's findings. The Llandwyn men were criticized for being off their station but praised for their subsequent bravery.

Happily the day when underpowered hulks, leaking at every joint, could put to sea are over now. Yet paradoxically the last 92-gunner ship of the time was wrecked in the Menai Straits as recently as 1953.

HMS Nile had been laid down at Devonport in October 1827. When she was launched twelve years later she was already obsolete. Although she was never to be commissioned as a sailing ship she did see active service. In 1854 she was used to blockade the Russian fleet in the Gulf of Finland. It was her only moment of glory. In 1867 she was towed to Liverpool where as *HMS Conway* she became a training school for Merchant Navy officers.

She did not see action again until the Liverpool blitz in 1941. An obvious fire hazard, she was moved first to Bangor and finally in 1949 to her last mooring in the Straits off Plas Newydd, the home of the Marquis of Anglesey.

The passage was a tricky one. She was the biggest vessel by far ever to pass through the Swellies but it was brought off brilliantly under the direction of two Caernarvon pilots, R. J. Jones and his son J. R. Jones, with two tugs holding the *Conway* steady fore and aft.

When, four years later, she was ordered to Birkenhead for a refit the first successful passage was used as a blueprint and at first it looked as though the earlier success was to be repeated. Both shores of the Straits were lined with hundreds of cheering spectators and more were ranged across the suspension bridge. The *Conway* was a stirring sight as she hove into view, bow waves curving like silver shavings, washing her black and white wooden walls.

Wreck of 'H.M.S. Conway' at Menai Bridge.

Henry Parry Collection, Gwynedd Archives Service.

As the crowds watched, the forrard tug steamed safely through the Swellies and passed under the bridge. It would be only minutes now before the crowds above her would watch the old veteran pass under their feet.

It was a sight they were never to see. Suddenly the *Conway* slowed to a halt. The tow line tautened and the watchers on the bridge saw the tug crews running to the sterns of their vessels. The *Conway* had been caught in the surge of an ebbing tide and it had brought her to a standstill. The tugs could not hold the old man-of-war. Slowly at first she began to drift backwards into the Swellies, dragging the tugs in her wake. Inevitably the tow line snapped and, her speed increasing, the *Conway* was drawn further into the wild water under the bank until finally with a great noise of rending timbers she ran aground. She was later and spectacularly set on fire.

At the far end of the Straits some years later there was another reminder of an earlier age.

In the mid-70's a dinghy sailor peacefully tacking off Abermenai was startled to see a puff of smoke from the terrace of Fort Belan followed by a bang. As he watched in mounting disbelief the ball continued its alarming trajectory until it buried itself in the sand on Abermenai uncomfortably near the head of a sunbathing holidaymaker.

The owner of both Fort and cannon, Lord Newborough — family motto 'Gentle in Manner, Vigorous in Action' — a hero of the Commando raid on St Nazaire who was later to escape from Colditz, was subsequently fined £25 for causing criminal damage. He told magistrates that the cannon had been loaded and fired without his knowledge during a party at his house.

The cannon was one of a pair recovered from a Spanish ship wrecked with great loss of life and treasure at Dinas Dinlle in the 18th century. It was not the first time it had caused trouble for its aristocratic owners. When the first Lord Newborough

48

The wreck of 'H.M.S. Conway'.

bought it in Victorian times he decided to test the cannon's fire power. Unfortunately it was loaded with too much powder. When it was fired every window in the Fort and every pane of glass in his hot houses was shattered.

The spoils of the Spanish ship seem to have carried a curse. Writing of the wreck a mayor of Caernarvon recalled an industrious tailor of Llandwrog who at an unusually low spring tide found a fortune in gold coins from the wreck in a rock pool. He filled the pockets of his drab top coat and breeches with so much money he could scarcely climb up the bank. Alas, the riches went to his head in the form of brandy fumes. No longer industrious he spent the fortune on drink and loose living and died in the workhouse at Caernarvon.

Lifeboats of Llandwyn

There had been a pilot station on Llandwyn Island since 1815. Eleven years later so great was the loss of life on the sandbanks of the Caernarvon Bar that a rescue boat was purchased by the Harbour authorities and the four pilots who lived on the island were conscripted to man her. The venture was not a success. There was neither boathouse nor slipway and the pilots were expected to manhandle their boat down the beach. Winter and summer, covered only by a length of matting, she filled with sand in any sort of a gale. It was hardly surprising the lifeboat was never launched. Finally in 1833 when the schooner *Staff of Life* broke up with the loss of all hands because the rescue boat could not be launched through shortage of crew, the station was closed and a new one opened in Caernarvon. This too proved useless. For most rescues on the Bar the boatmen were forced to beat against the prevailing wind. Then, in 1840, the Anglesey Life-Saving Association bought a six-oar Palmer class lifeboat from the RNLI for £78 payable over three years and the Caernarvon Harbour Trust built a boat-house and ramp on the island. Four extra hands were recruited from Newborough and a cannon shipped to the island to summon them to their oar.

The man behind this more practical approach was Sir Llewellyn Turner. A wealthy yachtsman who was mayor of Caernarvon for 11 years, Sir Llewellyn was a lifeboat 'buff', always happiest when he was himself taking part in rescues. He was one of the crew when, on October 18th, 1841, the Llandwyn cannon was fired for the first time. The fully-rigged sailing ship, *Mountaineer,* had gone aground on the North Bar flying an ensign reversed, the international distress signal. The crew, including the new extra hands from Newborough, took an hour to assemble after

51

the cox, G. Griffiths, had hoisted the ball to acknowledge the *Mountaineer's* signal. After launching, the boat battled for another half hour against a North-North-West gale at half flood with the sea running high.

The *Mountaineer,* bound for Liverpool from South America with a cargo of dye nuts, was stuck fast and rolling from bow to quarter. Six hundred feet windward of her coxswain Griffiths ordered the lifeboat anchor lowered and 60 fathoms of three-inch anchor cable were played out. Swinging on this axis the lifeboat veered until she came up alongside. In a heaving sea, lifted and hurled by the waves against the bulk of the *Mountaineer,* the lifeboat's gunwales were soon severely damaged but, though their boat twice filled with water, sixteen members of the crew were taken off. The seventeenth, a 17 year old boy, became deranged — and for an hour the lifeboatmen struggled with him on the pitching deck. But the boy had wrapped himself so closely in the rigging in his terror that he could not be extricated. Griffiths now had to make the decision that all RNLI coxswains dread. His lifeboat was taking a terrible pounding every time she was dashed against the side of the *Mountaineer.* Soon she would break up. The sacrifice of the life of the boy was the price of the safety of the men in his overcrowded boat. With the naked survivors, their clothes torn from them in the gale, huddled together for warmth in the open lifeboat he had no alternative but to order the crew to haul on the cable to bring the boat back over the anchor leaving the boy to his fate.

In such seas the task required almost superhuman strength and endurance. Wet, salt-caked rope scrapes skin from the horniest hands and there was the ever-present danger that the overcrowded boat would capsize in the heavy seas. At last the Llandwyn boat was almost over its anchor and Griffiths ordered the sail to be raised. the cable was cut and the lifeboat ran for Caernarvon.

Wreckage of the *Mountaineer* stretched along the shore from Llandwyn to Abermenai, amongst it the ship's six-foot tall figurehead, an officer in a Highland regiment. It was brought to Sir Llewellyn Turner's house, Parciau, and he bought it at once. He had been delighted at the success of 'his' lifeboat's first rescue and the figurehead became the pride of his collection of maritime mementoes. In wry old age he set this inscription at its side:

'This gallant officer filled a prominent position in the van in the good ship *Mountaineer* of Liverpool. After plowing the ocean for several years he shared the fate of the ship and was wrecked on Caernarvon Bar sixty years ago, when I had the honour of making his acquaintance. He was alternatively submerged and standing high in the air above water. As he did not avail himself of the service of the lifeboat David Jones threw him into his locker and with the vast wreckage of his ship he was landed by David upon the sand. His companions with the exception of a boy who perished in the lower rigging while trying to board the lifeboat were safely landed and this peaceful, well-behaved gentleman has resided at Parkia ever since and during this long period he has never tasted a drop of grog or spoken an unkind word either to his host or to anyone else.'

Five years later, in 1846, Sir Llewellyn and lifeboatmen from Llandwyn and Caernarvon were involved in another dangerous rescue.

The fully-rigged American ship *Soane* was in ballast to Bangor after discharging a cargo of grain in Galway when she was driven onto the North Bank.

The Llandwyn pilot's first attempt to launch into breakers higher than their heads ended in tragedy. They scrambled aboard only to be instantly capsized by huge breakers. One man was drowned and the lifeboat was swept away to be washed up two miles along the beach at Abermenai. All her oars were smashed.

By coincience, Sir Llewellyn and the crew of a Caernarvon boat had also beached at Abermenai. Taking command he decided there was no time to send for replacement oars. Plunging into the breakers he grabbed a broken blade and waving it over his head signalled to the crew of the *Soane* pointing first at the oar and then at the lifeboat. The Americans understood and pitched every available oar over the side. Enough washed ashore to enable the boat to be manned. But the onshore wind and heavy seas were still too strong to launch. Somehow the boat would have to be carried back to the launching beach at Llandwyn. Fortunately the plight of the lifeboatmen had been seen at the Ferry House at Tal-y-Foel. A team of horses was harnessed to a lifeboat truck and driven across the rough marshland of Newborough Warren; the lifeboat was lashed to the truck, and with the crews hanging on as best they might, the team galloped down the long beach to the island.

Sir Llewellyn, realising the Llandwyn men were exhausted, wanted his own crew to take the boat out but one of the Llandwyn pilots who had been in the capsized boat insisted on manning an oar. Unfortunately, it was soon obvious the earlier ordeal had robbed him of his nerve and the lifeboat had to turn back to put the frightened man ashore.

When, after the fourth launching, they came alongside the lifeboatmen found that the crew of the *Soane* had cut down the vessel's three masts. Held by the rigging the massive tree trunks bumped dangerously at the side of the ship.

Sir Llewellyn recalled:

'The masts alongside were like battering rams and I wondered why the crew had not cut them away. I fancy the reason was that if the ship went to pieces before aid came the floating masts might then be cut loose and some of the crew on them saved.

'On getting inside these battering rams the greatest nicety of steering was required. The fore and main masts were on the leeside and that was the best side for boarding the ship as the boat might be stoved in on the weather side.'

Fortunately the masts were far enough away from the lifeboat for her to be brought between them and the side of the ship and six hours after the first abortive launching the rescue began. Even to experienced seamen it was an alarming prospect. One moment the lifeboat was on the crest of a wave and level with the *Soane's* bulwarks, the next it had plunged to her keel. A man on the jumping ladder might easily be crushed to death between the two hulls yet, predictably, Sir Llewellyn was the first aboard. He even had time for an aesthetic judgement.

'The ship was thumping heavily, her stern striking the ground first,' he wrote. Then he added: 'When the ship's bows rose it was a beautiful sight to see the water falling from so great a length of the ship's anchor cables as the bows of the ship lifted them with it.'

One by one the frightened and exhausted crew were helped into the boat and finally put ashore. As a last flourish the *Soane* herself was rescued the next day. In quieter weather she was brought round on a kedge anchor into the shelter of Llandwyn.

The skeletal remains on Malltraeth sands of the Greek ship *Athena*—Master George H. Colscundi—remain as a memorial to the most hectic Christmas in the history of the Llandwyn lifeboat station. The *Athena* was carrying a cargo of beans from Alexandria to Liverpool when she ran aground in a south-westerly gale at 8 a.m. on 20 December, 1852. Coxswain Hugh Williams fired the warning gun and within half an hour the crew were assembled; clearly the drill had improved over the years. The boat was launched in Pilots' Cove in comparatively calm water but when she rounded the Point through the narrow neck of water into Malltraeth Bay the full force of the storm hit her, the sea filled the boat and the crew were lucky to get to shore with their lives. A launching from that side of the island was plainly out of the question. Soaked to the skin, the eight men lifted the 18-hundredweight boat onto their shoulders, manhandled her up the beach, over the headland and down the other side to Malltraeth Bay, only to find that there, too, launching was impossible. Once again a team of horses came galloping from Tal-y-Foel to drag the bumping lifeboat wagon behind them three-quarters of a mile along the beach to Malltraeth where four more volunteers were taken on so that each oar could be double manned.

By now the Greek crew were scrambling in the rigging waving caps, scarves, anything they could lay their hands on to signal their distress. But the breakers were so high that for the second time the lifeboat filled with water. Realising she would sink long before they could reach the *Athena*, Williams ordered his crew once again to return to the beach to bail out. This done, the boat was launched yet a third time and, rowing hard to the northward, they were at last able to put down an anchor and veer near enough to the *Athena* to get a heaving line aboard. Now it was the turn of the bowman. Held by his crew mates he perched in the bows gripping the knotter, a short rope attached to the Samson post, to steady himself. In his other hand he held a wooden rod with a loop at the end through which he would cast a two-inch thick heaving line with a grappling hook spliced on its end to give it momentum. Other hands paid out the life lines which would trail in the sea for swimmers to grasp but all work stopped when the bowman made his throw. The grappling iron, its rope tail whipping behind, soared through the air and the lifeboatmen watched with relief as it landed square on the *Athena's* deck. A man jumped down from the rigging, made the grappling iron fast and, hand over hand, the lifeboat's crew pulled themselves alongside.

One after another the Greeks dropped from the rigging into the lifeboat as she pitched below them. Some fell into the sea, grabbed the life lines and were in their turn hauled to safety. When all were aboard Williams brought the lifeboat astern of the *Athena*, ordered the line cut and the lifeboat dropped towards the shore.

Six days later the pilots' Boxing Day celebrations were interrupted when they were called out to rescue the crew of the Prussian brig *Die Krone*. The next day thirteen Russians were brought ashore to share the remains of the Christmas feast when their barque *Juno* ran aground.

Sir Llewellyn loved a rescue. When he saw a ship in distress he would take out any boat to link up with the Llandwyn crew though they did not always measure up to his high expectations.

When the brigantine *Meteor Flag* struck on the west angle of the South Bank of the Caernarvon harbour mouth in October 1870 Sir Llewellyn was so anxious to join the rescue that he put out in a boat wholly unsuited to the seas. Even the earliest lifeboats had grummets into which oars could be locked. Sir Llewellyn's craft had ordinary rowlocks and the sea constantly pitched the oars out of them. Yet somehow he managed to get abreast of the South Bank where the Llandwyn boat was lying at anchor. He assumed she had already taken the crew off the *Meteor* but, since he could only see two men, he clambered over the side and waded through the shoaling water to make sure all was well. Bearing in mind that he was in seas rough enough to ground a brig, his account of the adventure is a masterpiece of understatement. He wrote:

'I rightly guessed that the depth at that time of tide would not average more than about four feet. The distance and the gale prevented communication by voice. It was a curious undertaking and after a long struggle I found myself leaning on the gunwale of the Llandwyn lifeboat.'

The lifeboatmen—apart from the two on watch—were huddled out of the gale in the shelter of the bottom of the boat. Their reaction when a face peered at them over the gunwale is not recorded but Sir Llewellyn was furious. The watch had followed every yard of his perilous progress through breast-high seas. He wrote peevishly: 'I heartily wished that someone amongst them had possessed sufficient imagination to guess why a man should in cold weather take such a rash step, excepting to ascertain whether the crew were safe, as there are necessarily indentations on bar and sandbanks and wreckage that a man might tumble over.'

In 1860 the Palmer class lifeboat on Llandwyn was replaced by one of the RNLI's new 30-ft self-righting Peake class rescue boats. Four years later in the Great Storm of 1864 she proved her worth. The crew of the brig *Maria*, bound for Amlwch with a cargo of guano, were saved on the first day of the storm and on the second the crew of eight from the wreck of the schooner *Harry Russell* were taken to safety.

On 21 October, 1867, the crew of the Canadian barque *James Campbell* took to their boats when she hit the North Bank and they were transferred at sea to the Llandwyn boat which brought them ashore. On 3 December, 1867, the crew of four of the Amlwch brig *Monica* were saved.

Inevitably in such dangerous waters tragedy came at last to the lifeboatmen. On 24 January, 1874, five of them, in their other rôle as pilots, put off in a West-North-Westerly to take off a fifth man who had been piloting the schooner *Margaret*. The pilot boat reached her at 4.30 p.m. and the pilot transferred. It was the last time the four pilots and their two apprentices were ever seen alive though the body of one, John Jones, was washed up at Caernarvon the same night.

Ships from every maritime nation have come to grief off Llandwyn but it must be some sort of record that—not one but two—Canadian lake steamers should run aground in the same year, 1940. The first, in November, the *SS Eaglescliffe Hall*, had been running before a strong South-Westerly apparently out of control before she went aground in heavy breakers half a mile north of the island. None of the crew was injured. They were able to walk ashore on the ebb and four days later at high water after repairs to her steering gear the steamer was floated off undamaged.

The *Watkin F. Nesbitt*, a month later, was less fortunate. She drifted ashore in a westerly gale six cables length north of the island lighthouse striking the only rock on that stretch of beach with the loss of one life. But it was not the end for the *Nesbitt*. Salvage teams began to work on her as soon as the weather allowed. Her fore section—parts of which can still be seen on the foreshore—was cut away and the after section which contained the engine room was made watertight. Six months later the truncated ship was refloated and, after a hazardous tow without lights through the Straits where she went aground in Belan Narrows, she was towed to Birkenhead where her engine room was salvaged.

If Llandwyn Island produced heroes it also produced at least one villain according to a local story!

In the 18th century the beacon on Llandwyn which was the forerunner of the lighthouse was managed by an unprepossessing man named Evan Dhu. He was a man of middle height with massive shoulders and his evil reputation was enhanced by the black clothes he invariably wore and the dagger he carried in his waist belt. Petty crime seemed to follow him about. When he worked there as a rigger there had been a spate of petty robberies in Bangor which ended when he moved to Caernarvon.

Evan's job on the nights when high water was at midnight or when a westerly gale was blowing after sunset was to light a fire on the summit of the outermost cliff overlooking Porth Twr Mawr. To the authorities at Caernarvon he appeared to be doing his job admirably. Punctually at midnight on a high tide or at sunset in westerly gales the beacon would flame on Llandwyn. Yet, unaccountably, the number of shipwrecks increased. It was only when a party of local gentlemen managed to hide on the island that they discovered Evan Dhu's secret. By lighting the beacon to the north of the position it should have occupied, on the high land above which are now the pilots' cottages, he was able to lure ships onto the sharp jaws of Bird Rock to be pillaged at his leisure.

Wreck of the schooner 'Lilly' off Cemlyn in 1907.   Henry Parry Collection, Gwynedd Archives Service.

The steamer 'Matje' running ashore at Porthdinllaen.　Henry Parry Collection, Gwynedd Archives Service.

Robbers of the Rocks of Crigyll

The rusting weather-eaten carcass of a sea mine lies marooned in the Crigyll Estuary, and in the skies above the lonely dunes fighter bombers endlessly perfect techniques of aerial murder. A mile away Rhosneigr shelters behind superior semi-detached houses as though hiding from the Serpentine Crigyll as it twists through the Moor of Adders past the Golf Club and the Bay Hotel.

The Crigyll Estuary is a sinister place. Murder might easily be done there. And it has. Again and again. 'Robbers of the Rocks of Crigyll' has a ring about it of Ruddi-gore but there were no comic opera overtones to their bloody work over two and a half centuries.

They were never, it must be said, wreckers. There is no record that they lured un-suspecting ships with false beacons like Black Evan of Llandwyn. They had no need. The Crigyll Rocks, Ynys Wellt and Cerrig-y-Brain, reach out into the bay like a lobster claw and beyond them the sea breaks over a trip-wire of reefs. Vessels in plenty found the rocks unaided.

The Robbers came from almost every trade. At one time the gang included wealthy landowners, farmers, tailors, a weaver, a fuller, servants, housewives, even children. And on one occasion, at least, a group of Calvinistic Methodists were caught by an elder looting a wrecked ship.

Nor were the robbers without influence on the island. Even when customs officers caught them with the identifiable loot of ships hidden in their houses and fields it was almost impossible to get local magistrates to convict.

The robbers came mostly from the Crigyll parishes of Llanfihangel-yn-Nhywyn, Llechylched and Llanfaelog which in the 18th century, when the gang was most active, was a wilderness of sand dunes. But when word got abroad of a particularly rich wreck others came by boat from as far as Holy Island to join in the looting.

On new Year's Eve, 1740, the diarist Squire William Bulkeley of Brynddu on Anglesey recorded as he always did the island weather.

'The wind W. and by S. with a brisk gale fair and dry all day after sunrise but made heavy rain from 5 in the morning till 7 or 8, yet the snow is not quite yet.'

'Brisk' was probably not the word that George Jackson, the master of the Liverpool brigantine, *Loveday and Betty,* would have used to describe the gale that was driving his ship before it until finally with a rending of timber she ran aground on the Crigyll rocks.

Jackson was not greatly worried. His inspection showed that no great damage had been done and neither he nor his crew were injured.

After paying out a 90-fathom anchor cable to secure the *Loveday and Betty* and hiring a local man, Evan Owen, to guard the ship in his absence, he led his crew scrambling over the rocks to the shore. The nearest Excise office was at Aberffraw and by the time he arrived back the next morning with Peter Hughes, the tolls officer, the *Loveday and Betty* had been stripped of everything that could be moved.

The news of the wreck had not taken long to reach the robbers and by nightfall they had been swarming all over her. Encouraged by the guard, Evan Owen, Samuel Roberts, a Ceirchiog tailor, lowered the jib sail, folded it neatly and carried it ashore. Then he scrambled back on the deck and, with William Griffith Hughes of Llanbeulan, collected all the loose cable he could find and threw that into a cart which Rowland Humphreys had driven into the shallows in the lee of the *Loveday and Betty.*

It was soon obvious to Humphreys, who appears to have been the leader of the gang, that one cart was not going to hold all the booty. While the others went on

63

looting he went back up the beach to collect his brother-in-law, William Roberts, and three horses. The loot was loaded and taken to Humphreys' house where it was shared among the thieves.

More ropes were stolen by Gabriel Roberts of Ceirchiog who threw them down to his brother Thomas. As they made for home the guard, Evan Owen, called after them: 'If you don't make £100 tonight, you'll never make it!'

By dawn on New Year's Day there was very little left for the next team of thieves, Owen John Ambrose, who came on horseback from Llanfihgnel-yn-Nhywyn and John Pritchard who came on foot from Llanfaelog. Determined the day should not be a total loss, they cut the anchor rope and stole that leaving the *Loveday and Betty* at the mercy of the sea. It was to prove their undoing. They had barely got half a mile into the dunes before Captain Jackson and Hughes, the tolls officer, arrived on horseback and gave chase. Pritchard was the first to be captured but Ambrose, galloping wildly, gave them the slip. At the outskirts of Llanfihangel he put his horse down an embankment and had the satisfaction of watching his pursuers gallop past. It was a brief respite. A little way beyond his hiding place they stopped at the house of William Thomas. Ambrose heard them questioning a group of people and, as he listened, one of his neighbours denounced him.

It was too much for the robber. He ran up the embankment shouting: 'In the name of God, what shall I do?'

With two men captured it was not long before most of the gang were rounded up. Only Sam Roberts, the nimble tailor, and William Griffith Hughes escaped. They were never captured, but on 7 April, 1741, Ambrose, Gabriel Roberts, Thomas Roberts and Hugh Griffith Hughes stood their trial at Beaumaris Assizes. It proved to be a farce. William Chapple, the Chief Justice of Anglesey, was away and his

64

place was taken by Judge Thomas Martyn who was dead drunk during the entire proceedings.

William Bulkeley—himself a toper of no mean attainments—who attended the trial, was scandalised. That night he wrote in his diary:

'10th April. Tho this is the last day of the sessions the court sat to try causes till three in the evening: a thing never known before in the memory of man. Martyn the judge being every day drunk deferred all business to the last, when they were huddled over in a very unbecoming manner.'

As a result all the men from Crigyll were freed.

For nearly thirty years the profitable business of pillaging went on but there are no records of any of the Crigyll thieves being taken.

In 1742 Bulkeley recorded: 'They say that two ships are cast away S.W. of Holyhead but at Trefadog in Llanfaethlu a large West Indiaman is pounded to pieces and all the men perished but one Welshman who swam ashore: her ladeing was rum, sugar and cotton, the sugar was all melted by the sea, the casks of rum came ashore and the country people, they say, after drinking what they had a mind of knocked out the heads of ye casks and destroyed the rest.'

Only one mariner ever succeeded in getting justice and the barely credible story of how he won it is preserved in the Anglesey Sessions records.

The *Charming Jenny*, a single-masted 80-ton sloop, hit bad weather on 10 September, 1773, a day out of Dublin on passage to Waterford, Southern Ireland. Her captain and owner William Chilcott had his wife aboard. Perhaps thinking of her safety and that of his crew of two and a 19-year-old apprentice, Chilcott decided to abandon the voyage and run for the shelter of Holyhead. Within 24 hours the *Charming Jenny* had been pounded to kindling wood on the rocky flanks of Ynys Wellt. Her cargo, casks of red and white wine, Madeira, rum, brandy, beer and

Geneva gin to the value of £250, bedsteads, beds and bedding, cutlery and fine linen, bobbed in the breakers while the captain and his wife made their way across the rocks to the beach.

In the moments before they had struck, realising their danger, Mrs Chilcott had filled her pockets with her valuables and seventy guineas of her husband's money. The first to reach the beach, Chilcott saw his wife scrambling over the rocks, struggling against towering breakers. Too weak from the pounding he had taken from the sea to go to her aid he could only watch and pray. When he saw a figure scrambling over the rocks towards her Chilcott must have thought his wife was saved. A moment later he knew that he was wrong. According to one account, the figure grabbed his wife and a struggle began which ended with Mrs Chilcott's head being pushed into a rock pool until she drowned. When her body was examined later it was found that a finger had been broken in ripping off her wedding ring, the silver buckles had been torn from her shoes, her gold watch taken and the linen ripped from her body. And the money and valuables had gone.

To Chilcott, dazed with horror, the beach seemed filled with shouting men, women and children. Carts were galloped down the beach and horses followed dragging sledges. Farmers and their servants fought to secure the casks, breaking them with axes and swilling down the fiery spirits. Maddened by drink, one of the robbers came on the captain lying helpless on the beach. Taking out a knife he bent over Chilcott and began to cut away the silver buckles from his shoes.

Chilcott kicked out shouting, 'I'll know you again'. The robber ran off cursing. Much later Chilcott managed to crawl to the sand dunes where he found John Parry of Bryn-y-Bar sitting next to a cask from the *Jenny*. He asked Parry what he was doing.

'Damn you,' he was told. 'What is it to you? I am doing no more than what my neighbours are doing.'

Picking up a wooden stave Parry lunged towards the captain. Fortunately a farm servant, Moses Jones, came over the dunes and wrenched the stave from Parry's hand. Cursing, Parry picked up the cask and staggered off.

But the nightmare was not over. His ship wrecked, his wife murdered, his cargo scattered and looted, Captain Chilcott was forced to watch while one of the looters, William Williams, picked up the body of his wife and threw it into the cart. Struggling to his feet Chilcott staggered after the cart until it reached Williams's home. Williams plainly had no taste for murder. When he saw Chilcott he had him taken up to a bedroom where the captain lay, semi-conscious, for two days. It was an act of grudging charity which was to save his neck.

John Parry of Bryn-y-Bar, Rhoscolyn, had been one of the first to see the wreck when it went aground opposite his house. He had been binding corn with his maidservant Catherine Hughes, his servant John Owen and a neighbour, a tailor named Hugh Hughes from Pen-yr-Allt. Calling his daughter, Margaret, he took out a boat and all five were soon loading her to the gunwales with iron bedsteads, blue and white curtains and caskets of Madeira. Catherine concentrated on clothes, grabbing a dress, a black and white cotton and a white apron, all presumably the property of the captain's murdered wife. Back on shore the casks were buried on the beach and the other articles taken to Parry's house. For their second foray the Parrys and their helpers were joined by Owen Bentley, another Rhoscolyn man. Pausing on the deck to refresh themselves from a cask of Geneva gin which Parry broached with an axe they carried off an iron fender, more casks of wine and two bundles of iron bars. The plunder was taken to Bryn-y-Bar where it was shared and hidden under straw in a barn.

Obviously believing that a celebration was called for, Parry borrowed a horse and cart from William Williams of Carne and returned a third time to the *Jenny* that night to collect more casks which were drunk later by a party of eleven in the barn.

Not all the people on the beach that day were villains. John Owen, the servant to the Reverend Griffiths of Treban, was one of a party collecting driftwood. He was later to give evidence for the prosecution when the robbers were at last brought to trial. He deposed seeing William Williams and a fuller called William Roberts carrying a box of knives and forks up the beach. William Williams's own servant also gave evidence. He told how his master ordered him to bring a horse and sledge to the sea's edge where Williams loaded it with casks and pictures, two feather beds and a pair of chairs.

When news of the outrage at last reached the Revenue Officers they were too late to rescue the cargo but they moved the unhappy captain to Holyhead where leading citizens of the town crowded into his sick room to be appalled by the story he told.

A Justice of the Peace, John Griffiths, brought what must have been the most welcome news. He told Chilcott that warrants had been issued and a number of thieves had been found with the booty still in their possession. One, indeed, had already been found guilty.

A revenue officer, James House, searched the home of William Roberts, the fuller, and found the captain's sea chest containing his clothes and bank notes to the value of £195. Hidden under sacks the revenue man found a cask of Geneva gin, the brass fender, four pieces of white marble and four skeins of silk. At William Williams's house in Carne more casks were found and one of the silver buckles that had been ripped from Mrs Chilcott's shoe.

This pathetic reminder of his dead wife must have brought the night of the wreck vividly back to Captain Chilcott. Probably the only comfort he got was from the formidable pile of evidence against the men of Crigyll. As one after the other their guilt was established beyond question by witnesses to the outrage he must have felt that justice would soon be done.

He was to be a very disappointed man.

Two months after the shipwreck, still too ill and weak to walk, he was taken by carriage to the house of the magistrate John Griffith only to be told the case was being held over.

It was November before five Anglesey magistrates met in the Gwyndy Hotel, Llandrygarn, and then only two of the thieves, John Parry and William Williams, were committed to prison. Captain Chilcott was to assert that but for the support of the magistrates several more would have been arrested. In fact only one other man William Roberts, was ever committed to gaol.

At a subsequent meeting of magistrates several more warrants were issued. They were never executed.

A great crowd, friends and relations of the robbers, had gathered outside the hotel whilst inside the five magistrates wrangled bitterly. One magistrate, John Lewis, was so frightened he went home. Two of the others, John Griffith and William Lewis, left the room with the Clerk of the Peace, Ambrose Lewis, and in their absence orders were signed for the release of the three prisoners already in custody.

Back in the court room a furious row broke out which ended in the Clerk of the Peace knocking an attorney, John Williams, to the ground. William Lewis seemed about to join in the fracas. He began to unfasten his waistcoat buttons but thought better of it and instead ordered his servant to beat the attorney on his behalf. This was too much for the captain. Jumping to his feet he ran over to protect the attorney's back.

News of the fight reached the crowd outside the inn and it was all the constables could do to prevent the angry mob from bursting into the court so that they could attack the captain. Only with difficulty was he got away unharmed.

Determined to have justice, Chilcott next sought a writ of *habeas corpus* to have the trial moved to Shrewsbury where he thought he would have a better chance of a fair hearing. The only response was three summonses from John Griffith and William Lewis in February 1774 ordering the captain to appear before the Court of Quarter Sessions in Beaumaris to show cause why the prisoners should not be tried on Anglesey. His application for the case to be tried by the King's Bench was successful but the magistrates refused to pay the costs of the prosecution. Since Chilcott had lost everything in the wreck of his sloop it seemed an effective way to block the move but the captain was a determined man. Somehow he managed to borrow enough money to pay the legal costs and the travelling expenses of the prosecution witnesses to Shrewsbury and on 14 May, 1774, Roberts and Parry were remanded to Shrewsbury Gaol.

The first hearing in July was adjourned and a revised date set for 14 January, 1775. Once again Captain Chilcott had to meet the expense.

The Crigyll men's supporters made one last effort to prevent the trial. The writ of *habeas corpus* had specified that the accused should be tried in the nearest English county. Lawyers for Parry and Roberts submitted that Salop was not the nearest English county to Anglesey. Nor were Parry and Roberts idle on their own behalf. The *Shropshire Chronicle* on Christmas Eve, 1774, records an attempt by eight men to escape from their dungeon in the prison.

Stone masons' chisels were smuggled in to them and, covering the tips with stockings to deaden the sound, they tried to chip a hole in the dungeon wall. But they were discovered. On 14 January, 1775, the judges set aside the defence motion on the writ and on 22 March of that year Captain Chilcott had the satisfaction of hearing the sentence of death passed on the two men 'for the felony of stealing from the *Charming Jenny*'.

On 1 April Parry was hanged but nothing more is recorded of Roberts. Perhaps his belated charity in taking Chilcott into his home won him a reduced sentence of transportation.

Despite his victory, the captain was never to be wholly recompensed for the prosecution. In records of the Easter Sessions that year there is a note of the payment to him of £63 for his trouble and costs in bringing the action, £60 compensation for each trial and £12 for his travelling expenses to Shrewsbury. According to his own bill of costs the action had cost him altogether £350.

On the wall of the Jacobean court room in Beaumaris there is a plaster cameo. It shows a cow with one farmer pulling its ears, a second its tail and at its udder a solicitor sits milking the beast. Perhaps as he passed out of the court for the last time Captain Chilcott saw it and gave it a knowing smile.

The hanging of John Parry did little to curb the activities of his fellow looters and there was no shortage of opportunity. On 22 December, 1820, the ship *Jamaica* was smashed to pieces on the Crigyll rocks. On 5 December, 1830, two ships, the *Anne* from Plymouth and the *Active* out of Ipswich, ran aground. It was one of these ships the historian Gweirydd ap Rhys claims was looted by several leaders of the Calvinistic Methodists. They were alleged to have carried off 'some abundance of booty which was washed up by the tide'.

Naturally this extraordinary behaviour by some of the most respectable men on the island caused a great deal of comment. The matter was brought up at the

Monthly Meeting at Ty'n-y-Maen. Curiously no action seems to have been taken but it did bring about a shift in opinion against the looters of Crigyll. Articles began to appear in local newspapers criticising the robbers, usually under pseydonyms.

In 1831 the Reverend Samuel Roberts published an essay 'On the Cruelty and Odiousness of the Inhospitable Custom of Plundering Ships which have been Wrecked on the Sea-shore'. And in an Eisteddfod in 1842 in Bryngrawn, on the frontiers of Crigyll territory, the subject of the prize essay was 'The Wicked Custom of Stealing on the Sea-shores'. Seven competitors entered.

There were other inducements. In 1783 the Anglesey Druidical Society offered £10 to any farmer who helped to save life from a shipwreck. On 6 June, 1808, five men qualified when they saved the crews of the *Happy Return* and the *William Pitt*. And it was men from Crigyll families who helped a Rhoscolyn fisherman Hugh Davies save 102 lives during the 15 years he ran a one-man rescue service in his fishing boat.

Isolated acts of mercy did not mean that the Crigyll robbers had given up their profitable trade. On 30 October, 1867, their infamy even attracted the notice of *The Times*. Reporting the loss of the *Earl of Chester,* a stringer wrote:

'The wreck is now a prey to the notorious wreckers of the coast known to Welsh seafaring men as *Lladron Crigyll* (the Crigyll Robbers). Many hundreds of them were there yesterday stealing whatever they could carry away.'

Wreckage and cargo were strewn along the Crigyll beach for half a mile when the 493-ton *Earl of Chester* struck a rock at 7.30 on 28 October and sank with the loss of her ten passengers and crew, the master W. B. Nancollis and his wife. The *Earl* fired no gun, disaster must have overtaken the crew too quickly, and within half an hour she began to break up, less than a quarter of a mile away from the shore.

The alarm was raised by John Williams who lived on the beach at Rhosneigr but his action was to gain him scant thanks. Although there was no time to send to

Rhoscolyn, the nearest lifeboat station, Williams was to be criticised by the coroner William Jones who made scathing comments about the Rhosneigr folk who failed to go to the *Earl of Chester*'s aid. Hugh Hughes, an old seaman, rebutted the coroner. He remembered a total of 79 wrecks on the same rocks including the *Oakland* 13 years earlier, the schooner *Sea King* and the *Jane*. All had ended with terrible loss of life.

The wreckers had a busy night on that 29 October. A quarter of a mile from the *Earl of Chester* the Newfoundland brig, *Mountaineer*, struck and further up the coast the *Treuadra* floundered in Holyhead Bay.

There were only three coastguards along the whole stretch of coastline. When they had first heard the bell of the Newfoundlander they thought it was the bell for the watches on a passing steamer. A little later when they heard the *Mountaineer* grind into the rocks the alarm was sounded and the Rhosneigr lifeboat was launched with Evan Hughes as cox, and the chief coastguard, Sweeney, and 'four sons of honest Crigyll families' as crew.

After a frightening passage through the breakers the lifeboat managed to get within hailing distance of the *Mountaineer*. But there was no answer from her decks. It seemed certain that all on board were lost. There was nothing the lifeboatmen could do but return to the shore and await the arrival of rocket life-saving equipment which another coastguard, Lyons, had ridden to Holyhead to collect. At last it arrived and, watched by the lifeboatmen and the crowds on the beach, Lyons assembled it, a desperate task on an exposed headland in a fierce 'blow'. The first shot landed square on the ship's deck. Everyone waited but there was still no sign of life. It was only when the disappointed rescuers came up the beach that they were told the entire crew of the *Mountaineer* were safe. They had come ashore in their own boats.

Wrecks and Rescues

On 29 March, 1883, Crigyll folk took part in a rescue which did much to counterbalance their evil reputation.

The 855-ton *Norman Court* was built as a clipper for the tea trade. She had raced the *Cutty Sark* and most of the famous clippers of her day; once she had brought her cargo of tea back to Britain in a record time of 96 days, but, her days of glory over, she was re-rigged as a barque carrying a cargo of sugar from Jamaica when she ripped out her bottom on the Crigyll rocks.

The force of the impact brought the mainmast crashing down, sending the lifeboats spinning from their davits like bath toys. The crew could be seen from the shore clinging to the mizzen rigging crying for aid.

The Rhoscolyn lifeboat, the nearest to the wreck, was out of service in Trearddur Bay where she was undergoing repairs. Five attempts to fire rocket lines failed as one after another the rockets were deflected by the force of the wind or fell short, spluttering their life out as they hit the sea. At last the Rhosneigr lifeboat was launched though there seemed little doubt the crew were being sent to their deaths. First they faced the danger of capsize in the huge breakers that were pounding the shore, then they would have to traverse two reefs heading upwind between rocks and shoals in a boiling sea through breakers the size of houses. Yet somehow, with their boat curvetting, the crew managed to bring her under the barque only to be struck as they rounded the stern by a terrifying wave which lifted them high in the air. One man was swept overboard in the rush of water that filled the boat but he managed to save himself by grabbing a lifeline and hanging on until the wave passed and his crew mates were able to drag him to safety.

Two more attempts were made to get round the stern to the jumping ladder amidships but each time the boat was thrown back on the curved crests of waves that tossed her into the troughs behind. Exhausted by heavy seas, blinded by flying spume, at last they had to give up and let the seas carry them back to the shore to rest before making a further attempt. By the time they beached, a crowd had gathered—and when the next launch was made men and women waded up to their waists in freezing seas to steady the lifeboat until she could be got under way. Once again, bending to their oars, their eyes stitched together by glistening threads of ice, the lifeboatmen came up on the *Norman Court* and once again they were hurled away by taunting, bullying seas.

Colonel Marshall, the Rhoscolyn Lifeboat Secretary who had been watching the plight of the *Court,* realising the boat's crew were at the end of their strength, chartered a special train to bring a boat and crew from Holyhead to Rhosneigr. Manhandling their boat across the moor and down the beach the new crew managed to launch and came up alongside the stricken vessel just as the Rhosneigr men, collapsing by this time with exhaustion, were returning to the shore.

The new boat had arrived just in time. When at last the Holyhead crew boarded the *Norman Court* they found her crew so numb they had to be prized from the rigging like frozen washing.

March 1883 was a significant month for the people of the coast. A single coastguard with an armful of rockets achieved what coastguards and revenue men over two and a half centuries had failed to accomplish. He ended the bloody tradition of the Crigyll Robbers.

Coastguard John O. Williams was no ordinary man. Born in Pembroke in 1844, he joined the Royal Navy and transferred to the coastguard service when his time expired. He went to Rhosneigr after valiant service at Holyhead. He was the holder of

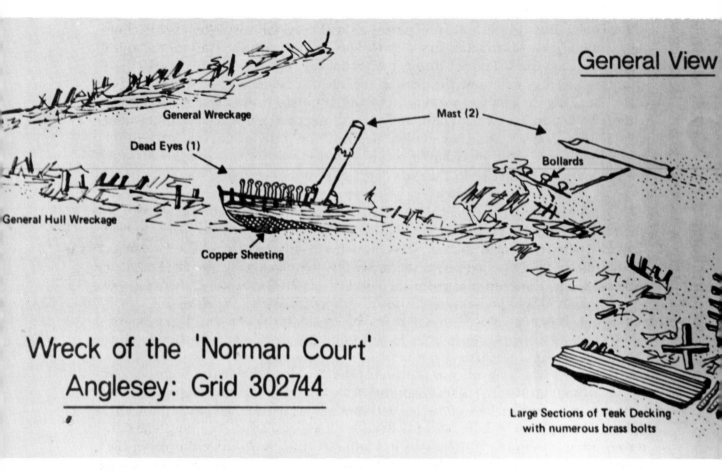

General Wreckage

Mast (2)

Dead Eyes (1)

Bollards

General Hull Wreckage

Copper Sheeting

Wreck of the 'Norman Court'
Anglesey: Grid 302744

Large Sections of Teak Decking
with numerous brass bolts

RAF divers' view of the wreck of the 'Norman Court'.
76

Gwynedd Archives Service.

twelve life-saving awards and an expert with rocket apparatus. When storm cones were hoisted it was his practice to set up rockets on the beach and wait for the sound of approaching ships. His action on 1 March, 1883, is typical of his work.

Shortly after 3 a.m. he saw the port light of a vessel bearing down on the Crigyll rocks. He fired two warning rockets and had the satisfaction of watching the brig *Elizabeth Kloustebere* veer out of danger. Later, a second ship was saved in the same way by his rockets but, shortly before dawn, there was the sound of timbers rending on rock and the lifeboat was launched. The crew found only one survivor, a Dutch seaman, Jacob Biering. To Williams's dismay he gave the name of his ship. It was the *Elizabeth Kloustebere*. They had seen the warning rocket and missed the rocks but in the dark, in strange waters, they had drifted round in a circle and the second time round they struck.

During his service at Rhosneigr Williams saved so many lives with his rockets that the men of Crigyll paid him a curious back-handed compliment. In 1878 an inspection of naval reserves by Admiral Sir Augustus Philimore was interrupted by a deputation of Crigyll farmers. Could the Admiral use his influence, they asked. Williams was taking away their living by warning off vessels with his rockets!

*　　*　　*　　*

RAF Rhosneigr had a chilling reputation in the 1940's. Sited behind sand hills thirty feet high and the landing strip little more than packed sand, the station had a higher casualty rate than the Battle of Britain squadrons. Drifting sand clogged the engine filters and intakes of the Spitfires and Hurricanes. The life between major overhauls of the Rolls Royce Merlin engines was only 50 hours. Often they failed miles out in the Irish Sea on the squadron's convoy patrols. There were no air-sea rescue launches, no helicopters, in the early days of the war. Even the crews of aircraft which came down yards from the shore had small hope of survival.

At 11.30 a.m. on 28 August, 1941, a Botha twin-engined bomber with a Polish crew of three crashed in the breakers immediately after take-off. The Botha had taken off in weather in which no aircraft should have flown but a convoy was being attacked by a U-boat and operational necessity overcame common sense. A full south-westerly gale was blowing up towering waves which crashed over the bomber and sent clouds of spray halfway across the airfield. A lifeboat secretary who saw them described them as 'moving walls of water'. The sea was so wild that the Porth Dinllaen boat took an hour and a half in heavy seas to make the short passage across Caernarvon Bay. Meanwhile RAF ground crews and young soldiers from the station anti-aircraft battery reached the beach in time to see two of the aircrew swept to their deaths.

A coastguard, Evan Jones, and Aircraftsman 1st class Albert Atkinson were the first to take a boat out. Warned by local men of the danger Jones replied simply: 'It's my duty to try.'

Within minutes the boat had capsized, Jones was drowned and Atkinson was swept onto the shore barely alive. Yet almost at once the 29-year-old village policeman, George C. Arthur, and a Merchant Navy second officer Arthur J. Owen who had arrived on leave the day before to attend his father's funeral, called for seven volunteers to man a whaler they had found on the beach. The officer in charge of the A.A. unit, Second Lieutenant Peter Whysall, his Battery Sergeant Major Alfred Moger, Sergeant Charles Jackson and three gunners stepped forward.

When they tried to launch the whaler the breakers knocked them spinning, ripping the boat out of their hands and hurling it back up the beach, but at length they succeeded in climbing the surf in the pitching craft. Owen ordered them to row out to sea beyond the breakers and then to come about and approach the aircraft from the calmer waters beyond. But as they came under the lee of the plane they were hit by a beam sea and the boat capsized. There were only three survivors, Sergeant Jackson, Lance Bombardier Tommy Taylor and Gunner Jack Parkinson. P.C. Arthur's body was washed ashore shortly afterwards still wearing his steel helmet; Owen's, the Merchant Navy officer, was found several days later. At least two other boats were launched but both capsized almost at once hurling their occupants into the breakers. Two bombers from RAF Rhosneigr which had by this time joined in the resuce dropped life-jackets to them as they fought for their lives. But it was no use. The breakers caught the life-jackets and swept them out of reach. Frantic at the plight of their comrades, fourteen soldiers and airmen swam out to rescue them. Four were drowned almost at once and the others only regained the shore with difficulty.

An eye-witness who had been watching through binoculars said later:

'There were men struggling in the water everywhere. It was heart-breaking and people on the head were crying openly. There were hundreds of people watching. The sea was so high that it seemed impossible anyone could be rescued. At times the small boats could be seen on the crest of huge waves. Then came a shout and it could be seen then that the boat had capsized and the men had been thrown in the sea. Some tried to swim out to them in an attempt to rescue but the high waves were stronger than they were. Later there was a shout. One of the men was nearly reaching the shore and a soldier braved the rough seas to reach him. It was the policeman, Arthur, but in spite of every attempt to revive him he died. By this time almost everyone was in tears. In a short while there was another shout and it was seen a man was being tossed to and fro by the waves. Again the same brave soldier went into the sea and brought him ashore. It was one of the crew of the aircraft. He too was dead.'

Two 17-year-old holidaymakers, Stuart Wood from Chester and his friend Derrick Boynham, were looking at the uninspiring wartime menu in a cafe in Rhosneigr when they heard about the bomber. Their hunger vanished as they ran out of the cafe down to the beach where they commandeered a boat.

Recalled Derrick: 'We could hear people shouting, warning us not to put to sea but we decided we must have a go.'

The two youngsters managed to launch the dinghy in the explosion of surf, climb aboard and row until they were within five yards of the aircraft. It took three quarters of an hour to row less than 200 yards.

Said Derrick: 'We could see three airmen clinging to the fuselage. They called out that they were very weak. We made signs for them to get into the boat but at that moment a huge wave struck, washing two of the airmen away and capsizing the dinghy. I managed to climb onto the wing of the aircraft but I was immediately swept away and I had to hang onto the upturned boat. She was continually being turned over and over by the rough sea. Once I was trapped underneath but luckily a wave turned her over and freed me.'

Stuart Wood had also managed to cling to the upturned boat. Now the two boys swam back to the fuselage where the solitary Pole was crouching terrified. Pausing only to get their breath they persuaded him to try to crawl along the wing to their boat which was rapidly drifting shorewards. At any moment they knew the aircraft might sink dragging them and the RAF man with it.

The Pole who had been slightly injured in the crash was weak from shock and exposure and scarcely able to help himself. The boys had to drag him from the wing into the sea. Battered by punishing waves and weakening themselves, the two nevertheless managed to keep their heads above water and support the man as they swam after their boat. So strong were the seas that the aeroplane, too, was being pushed to-

80

A helicopter from RAF Valley demonstrating a modern rescue at sea while the crew of an off-shore inflatable stand by.

A Neilson Photograph.

wards the shore. At length they reached their boat and grabbed at it with almost their last strength. Using now an oar, now the upturned boat, sometimes the aeroplane itself for support, the boys managed to keep themselves and the airman afloat. As they drifted towards the shore they were washed past one of the beach defence posts which in wartime were driven into the shallows round the coast of Britain to repel invaders. One of the boys grabbed one and put the Pole's hands round it. Then, since the slender wood was not strong enough to bear their combined weight, he gallantly swam back into the breakers. By now both boys were so weak they had given up hope of ever reaching the shore until they saw spectators form a human chain. As the boys swirled past, the leading 'link' succeeded in seizing them and passed them onto the beach. The Pole was less fortunate. Although well within his depth at the post he was too weak and exhausted to realise where he was. As the human chain moved out towards him he lost his grip, was swept away and drowned.

In all, fourteen people lost their lives in what was surely one of the most stirring human dramas ever played out around the island coast.

For their efforts the two boys were awarded George Medals and the RNLI silver medal for gallantry. They both received autographed silver cigarette cases from General Sikorski, Commander-in-Chief of the Polish Forces. Among the survivors from the boats Sergeant C. Jackson, Lance Bombadier T. Taylor, Gunner J. W. Parkinson and Aircraftsman 1st class Albert Atkinson won RNLI bronze medals.

Posthumous bronze medals were also awarded to Second Lieutenant Peter T. Whysall, R.A. Battery Sergeant Major Alfred W. Moger, Gunner Clarence H. Thornton, Second Officer Arthur J. Owen, M.N., Police Constable George C. Arthur, Coastguard Officer Evan Jones and Gunner Reginald Eaton. All the swimmers received Royal Humane Society medals. Perversely, at Rhosneigr there is no plaque on the sea wall to recall their gallantry.

According to legend, the most curious fleet that ever made a landfall on the stretch of beach between Rhoscolyn and Trearddur Bay was the flotilla of turfs which brought St Ffraid and her hand-maidens from Ireland fleeing from Ffraid's father, an Irish king, who sought to make her marry against her will. The savage coast around Trearddur is a place of legend and folk tales. None is more poignant than the legend of Betsy's Cave and the true story of a dog called Tyger.

Big Betsy and her husband Little Dick were small holders. When their son ran away to sea they found it difficult to make their land pay and they turned to looting wrecked ships, hiding their booty in a cave which had a natural rock platform at the far end.

Looting proved more profitable than farming; never more so than the night a ship carrying a cargo of cases of whisky ran aground at Rhosneigr. The beach was littered with bottles, and Betsy soon had twelve stuffed down the legs of her capacious bloomers. Clanking noisily, she scurried up the beach to the cove—leaving her husband behind to make his own collection. Little Dick, lacking the hiding places his wife could command, smuggled much of his whisky internally and his progress up the beach was slow and uncertain in consequence. But the sight which met him when he reached the cave sobered him at once. Collapsed at the foot of the rocky platform was his wife. Above her on the platform was the body of their sailor son. A member of the crew of the whisky ship, he had drowned in the wreck and his body had been washed into the very cave where his parents kept their contraband.

The story of Betsy's cave may be insubstantial folklore but proof of the dog Tyger's bravery is preserved in stone. His epitaph 'Tyger Sept 17, 1819' is carved in the cliff above the Black Arch in the south-eastern corner of Penrhos Bay.

Tyger was a retriever, the pet of the skipper of a ketch which struck a rock, Maen Piscar, in fog and sank in deep water. As she went down Tyger barked at the crew and then, jumping into the sea, began to swim vigorously. The captain and his crew, two men and a boy, although they could see nothing through the fog, trusted to the dog's instinct and jumped in after him, the boy clinging to Tyger's collar.

It was a long swim and by the time the party had reached the breakers all the men were exhausted. But as they prepared for death they had the consolation of knowing that at least the boy was safe. Through a break in the fog they could see the dim outline of Tyger dragging him above the high-water line. Then, to their amazement, Tyger leapt back into the sea and swam towards them. As the dog came near, the captain waved to the weakest sailor and Tyger, understanding, swam towards him. Soon he too was being pulled out of the sea while the captain supported the other member of the crew. His own strength was failing but he kept afloat until he felt Tyger pushing at his arm. Pulling the seaman's hand through the dog's collar the skipper once more waved Tyger back to the beach trying weakly to swim behind. He had reached his limit when out of the fog came Tyger and, side by side, the dog pushing and encouraging his master, they eventually reached land. But the effort had been too much—even for Tyger's great heart. With a final reassuring lick of his master's hand he collapsed on the beach and died.

There was a lifeboat station at Rhoscolyn for twelve months short of a century. During that time two names dominated its history, that of its most famous cox, Hugh Hughes, and the two lifeboats which were successively named *Ramon Cabrera*.

Hughes had a magnificent record as a lifesaver even before he joined the RNLI. Using his own fishing smack and a volunteer crew of Crigyll men he saved twenty four men from a sailing ship in 1866, ten from a Newfoundland brig in 1867, eight from one Spanish barque, five from a second and ten from an English schooner in 1874, twenty from a Spanish ship in 1875 and fifteen from an English barque in 1881.

The first *Ramon Cabrera* and the lifeboat house in which she was kept had been the gifts in 1878 of the Countess de Morella who named the boat after her first husband. It was nine years later before the boat went out on her first service, to the Norwegian barque *Hjemlos*, sinking with her crew of eight in Cymyran Bay. But it was the second *Ramon Cabrera*, a larger boat with Hugh Hughes as cox, that on December 8, 1901, in a whole gale from the north-west by west made the first of the station's epic rescues.

The schooner *J. W. Wearing* was in difficulties six miles west of Rhoscolyn Point when the lifeboat launched. Three times the bowman, balancing in the prow while the oarsmen attempted to hold the pitching boat steady, threw a line to the vessel. Each time it fell short. Then, as he poised for a fourth attempt, a wave sent the *Cabrera* rocking on her beam ends. Before her crew could right her she began to fill with water. Only by hurling themselves against the yaw of the boat, thus emptying her of water, did the crew save themselves from drowning.

A fourth line landed on the *J. W. Wearing's* deck only to snap like twine the instant it was made fast. More lines were thrown until finally first one held and then a second one was made fast. It was a brief victory. The first two seamen had barely swung down them to safety before yet again they snapped.

The *J. W. Wearing* was now within 200 yards of Porth Saint rock yet, though it exposed the lifeboat to the full force of the gale, Hughes brought her under the *Wearing's* stern. Pitching in the heavy seas, the *Ramon Cabrera* took a terrible buffeting. Again and again she was hurled against the side of the *Wearing* until five oars were lost and the sixth driven through the side of the boat trapping the mast. At

85

once a local fisherman, George Smith, seized an axe and with a single blow severed the oar freeing the mast. When they had taken off the remaining three crewmen the lifeboat, clearing the rocks by a boat's length, made for home. Behind them the *J. W. Wearing* was smashed to matchwood in ten minutes.

The other great service performed from the Rhoscolyn station was on December 3, 1920. The *Timbo*, a tiny coastal 'puffer' out of Whitby in ballast and bound from Liverpool to Newport, South Wales, was caught in a north-easterly gale. Blown before the wind, she was driven off course into Caernarvon Bay. The windows of the wheelhouse were blanketed with snow, her decks sheets of ice, and as the crew slithered across them to send up distress signals the gale cut at their faces like a cutlass.

When the Rhoscolyn boat came up on the *Timbo* she was tossing on her stern anchor chain, a kite in the wind, and no sooner did the oarsmen bring the lifeboat under the ladder amidships than a fresh wave washed them away again. The bowman's lines either fell short or, if they reached the deck and were made fast, the enormous tension as the two craft yawed in opposite directions snapped their 3-inch cables as easily as sewing thread. Yet, soaked to the skin, frost gumming their eyes, the cuts on their faces where they rubbed with salt-caked hands smarting under the bite of the salt, the crew bent to their oars.

Lifted to the crest of waves high as houses and then plunged from a terrifying height into desolate troughs, the lifeboat crew were in greater danger than the men on the coaster. Her anchors were holding but Owen Owen, the 'cox', read the exhaustion in the faces of his own crew. He knew that they must make for the shelter of the lee shore at Llandwyn or be lost.

For an hour the *Cabrera* beat against the wind until a wave, bigger than any that anyone in the boat had ever seen, crashed over the prow. Two of the crew, Evan

Hughes and Owen Jones, were swept up by the rush of water and hurled over the side to their deaths.

The survivors were now fighting for their own lives. The lifeboat was taking a terrible pounding. The sea seemed to go mad. Wave after wave of freezing water crashed over the crew. Desperately frightened, they grabbed lifelines and huddled low in the boat to get what cover they could. They were being blown further and further from the lee shore, their only hope of safety. Then, two miles from land, a second monstrous wave sent the boat skittering along the sea's surface on her beam ends, her mast yawed wildly, the sail filled with sea water and Coxswain Owen, William Thomas and Richard Hughes were thrown into the sea and drowned.

In the graveyard at Rhoscolyn there is a moving memorial to commemorate their deed but the heart had gone out of their successors and nine years later the station was closed down.

'S.S. Dakota' wrecked on East Mouse, Bull Bay, September 1877. Lifeboat saved 20 lives.
Gwynedd Archives Service.

Wreck of the Portmadoc schooner 'Owen Morris', 1907. Henry Parry Collection, Gwynedd Archives Service.

88

Wreck of the steamer 'Missouri' off Holyhead.   Henry Parry Collection, Gwynedd Archives Service.

The Scary Skerries

There has been a warning light on the Skerries since 1713 when Queen Anne licensed William Trench, an Irish entrepreneur, to erect a 35-ft high beacon which burned 100 tons of coal a year and to collect 1d per ton from each vessel that benefited from its light. It was not a successful venture. Although he only paid a rent of £20 a year to William Robinson of Gwersyllt and Mynachdy, the owner of the island, Trench died in penury and his son was drowned ferrying coal to replenish the beacon. Cannier descendants won permission to double the toll, though for foreign vessels only, and in 1804 a relative by marriage of the Trenches, a Welshman named Morgan Jones, replaced the coal beacon with an oil lantern. In 1810 Mr Jones had the forethought to buy the islands from the Robinsons for an undisclosed sum. It was a shrewd move. By 1828 the Port of Liverpool was being used by an enormous quantity of shipping and the annual income from the lighthouse had reached £11,800 a year.

In 1835, Trinity House was empowered by Parliament to take in hand all the private lighthouses in Britain. Morgan Jones's nephew (another Morgan, who had inherited the kindly light with an annual revenue of £23,000 a year) turned down Trinity House's first offer of £300,000. By 1840 it was the last privately-owned lighthouse in Britain, and pressure was increasing on the family to sell out. In 1841 a special jury sitting in Beaumaris fixed a price of nearly £500,000 for the light—of which two-thirds went to the Jones family and a third to the Robinsons who, little more than a century earlier, had no doubt thought they had struck a hard bargain when they rented the island for £20 a year.

The Robinsons never had any luck on the Skerries. Newly-wed William Robinson, the grandson of the man who had leased the island, arrived on Anglesey to inspect the estate he had inherited. With him he brought a neighbour from the mainland called Edward, his gardener, two servants—one of them John Lewis the father of a week-old boy—and the young son of the other servant. Landing for a picnic on the Skerries they met another group of young 'bloods', squires' sons William Watkin, Richard ap Sion ab William Probert and Richard Owen ap William Bedward.

The two parties joined up, debauch was soon under way and no one noticed that a storm was brewing. When they did notice they were too drunk to care and made ready to cast off their boat the *Mary*.

One of the servants' boys was so terrified at the prospect of sailing through the storm across the tide rip that he ran away and hid in a pile of straw. For a while the 'bloods' hunted him, spearing the straw with pitchforks, but luckily for him they tired of the sport and launched the boat without him.

A contemporary wrote of the weather in which they launched: 'The wind blew so high and rained so fast withall that ye people in the Island soon lost sight of them.'

When they did not arrive on the mainland it was at first hoped that they had been blown to the Isle of Man and a boat was dispatched by Robinson's family to look for them there. For weeks reports of sightings were followed up by the heart-broken relatives—and advertisements were placed in newspapers all over the north-west coast.

At last from Whitehaven came news that a boat 'empty and miserably broken' containing the lid of a wooden box bearing the name of one of the party had been found in a creek near the town. The oars, the rudder and the foremast were missing and the main mast and sails were heaped in the bottom of the boat.

The contemporary wrote: 'Of 13 persons most of them members of families and fathers of small children not one is to be found alive or dead . . . lost in following the caprice of a hot-headed young gentleman.'

In March 1675 the Right Honourable Joseph Williamson, Principal Secretary of State to Charles II, received this despatch from John Anderton from the Crown Office in Chester Castle.

'That the *Mary* yacht is certainly ship-wrecked I have it from the mouths of two gentlemen that escaped from aboard her who relate thus:

'On Thursday the 25th instant about two o'clock in the morning in foggy weather the ship launched upon a rock to the N.W. of the Skerrys that lie to the Eastward of the Bay of Holyhead. The seamen and the passengers were for the most part snug under decks. The first touch raised the seamen who cried all was well but immediately the ship struck upon another rock and there sank. The Skerrys is a small isle—an appendage to Anglesey about a league from the shore. The rock on which the ship struck was so near land that when the sea made the ship roll the mast touched land by which only means of escape lives were preserved.

'The Earl of Meath and about 34 more perished in the ship whereof the master Captain Burslow, the Boatswain and two more sailors were of this number. The master and 23 mariners with 15 passengers got safe upon the island. Amongst the 15 passengers were the Earl of Ardgloss and Lord Ardee, son of the Earl of Meath and now his father's successor in the family estate.'

The captain who bravely went back to lead the Earl of Meath across the mast lost his own life in the attempt. The despatch continued:

'It was 12 noon on Thursday at Noon on the 25th instant before the mast gave way—the captain to save the Earl of Meath and the rest lost himself.

'The preserved were on the island from Thursday morning until Saturday afternoon and had relief by a flask of gunpowder by which they struck fire with a steel and of the wreck boards of the ship made a fire. Now they roasted some mutton but had no bread nor any liquid but salt water till providence cast ashore a small cask of whisky which they divided proportionate among themselves.

'A Wicklow vessel from Beaumaris went as near the Isle as she durst and took in the 15 passengers and 24 seamen and landed them on Sunday last at Beaumaris which is the most particular account I can give you of this sad accident . . .'

The *Mary* occupies a unique place in British maritime history. She was the first Royal Yacht and in her Charles II originated the sport of yacht racing, against his brother the Duke of York.

'Jachts' (the word means Hunter) had recently made their appearance in the Dutch Navy of the day. Light and fast they were used in wartime as patrol boats and in peacetime, luxuriously appointed, they carried the nobility round the country along the network of canals.

When Charles II, exiled in Holland, was restored to the English throne he made the journey from Breda to Rotterdam in a 'jacht' owned by the Prince of Orange.

It was love at first sight, and the burgomaster of Amsterdam was left in no doubt when he was presented to that merriest of monarchs that a 'jacht' would be the perfect present for a king who had come into his own.

The hint was taken. The *Mary* was purchased from the Dutch Admiralty, fitted out by the country's finest craftsmen and with a smaller yacht, the *Bezan*, sailed to England under a Dutch seaman, Captain John de Groes, 'a symbol of the esteem in which the citizens of Amsterdam hold the king'.

Captain de Groes was immediately commissioned into the Royal Navy and the *Mary* became the ancestor from which the thousands of sailing dinghies and racing yachts which sail round Britain today are descended. She was, in fact, the first yacht to be owned or sailed outside Holland.

Unhappily her shallow draught made the *Mary*, designed for canals as she was, unsuitable for the rougher English waters. Experiments with stone ballast proved unsuccessful and in 1661 Charles ordered another modified yacht, the *Katherine*, and the *Mary* was drafted into the Royal Navy. For 15 years until she broke up on the Skerries she was used to transport high officers between Dublin and Holyhead.

Incredibly, for three hundred years, this unique vessel lay undisturbed on the sea bed. But for the merest chance she might be there yet.

On July 11, 1971, a party of divers from the Chorley and Merseyside branches of the British Sub-Aqua Club diving for lobsters were driven by a change of weather onto new ground. On the first dive they came upon the *Mary's* four bronze cannons.

An ex-Naval tug, the *Francis Sea*, was borrowed from the Bootle Barge Company and a team of experienced divers assembled under marine archaeologist P. N. Davies.

Meanwhile the delicate work of cleaning the four cannons began—revealing them as the finest examples of matching bronze 17th century armaments ever discovered.

The problem of recovery from the wreck are enormous. So dangerous are the waters in which the *Mary* lies that, although she is only 14 metres below the surface, diving can only take place in the summer and then only for an hour each side of slack water. Nevertheless, an impressive collection of artefacts has been recovered in the last six years. It includes two hundred silver coins, Captain William Burslow's pewter plate marked with his initials W.I.B., his silver spoon and fork, a heavy gold signet ring, another ring with an imitation jewel, a set of weights and several silver candlesticks. In 1975 a more macabre find was made when the bones of two people, one of them a girl of about 20, were found buried under the wreck.

There was a curious echo of the wreck of the *Mary* on 12 October, 1841, when the 229-ton brig *Dido* struck the west coast of the Skerries.

The *Dido*, under her master Captain Carpenter, was returning from the Bight of Benin fully laden with a cargo of hogsheads of palm oil and bags of gold dust which were never recovered.

The nine-month voyage had been ill-starred from the beginning. While they were still in the Benin Roads a dispute had arisen between the 33-year-old mate William Tatham and the second mate Edward Hills. It ended with Tatham stabbing Hills to death and spending the rest of the long voyage in irons. In the heat of the tropics such a confinement must have been agonizing but worse conditions awaited as they neared the port of Liverpool. Off Bardsey the *Dido* fell victim to winds of hurricane strength. Her mainyard and fore-topsails were first ripped into shreds, then blown completely away so that the brig was driven before the wind and seas. She struck at 10 p.m. but fortunately her jib boom rammed into a rock crevice creating a bridge over which the master and crew, twenty eight in all, tight-roped to dry land. All but two succeeded. By coincidence both were medical men, Morgan, who was the ship's doctor, and a passenger called Read.

Fifteen minutes after the last man stepped onto the rock the vessel broke up under the pounding of the surf. The following morning the sea for miles around was sprinkled with hogsheads of palm oil but by that time the crew were safe. Boats from Holyhead had answered the 'ship in distress' signal put up by the Skerries Light. The luckless mate Tatham was brought under escort to Holyhead and from there committed to the County Gaol.

The log book of the Stanley Sailors' Home at Holyhead gives a list of the ship-wrecked mariners who arrived there for succour. During the winter months at the turn of the century scarcely a night seems to have passed without refuge being

95

sought by the crew of some stricken ship. Usually the entries are brief, almost laconic. But occasionally accidents happened so bizarre as to require elaboration . . .

'At 2 a.m. on January 8th 1905 14 men from the steamers *Stella Maria* and the Spanish steamer *Orion* were brought to this home. Their vessels had been in collision off the Skerries. The *Stella Maria* sinking at once her crew were saved by jumping on board the *Orion* and making for Holyhead. When about threequarters of a mile from the breakwater the *Orion* foundered and the men took to the boats. One boat with 14 men in was picked up by a lobster boat that happened to be at the breakwater and were landed. The other boat with 12 men made for the Skerries. As they only had one oar, with fair wind and tide they arrived at 5 p.m.

'In the meantime the steam lifeboat was searching for them off the Skerries and brought them to Holyhead about 2 a.m., both crews losing all their effects.'

There were twenty six men in all and in the words of the logbook: 'Everything was done for them when they arrived. They were all supplied with an outfit by the Shipwrecked Mariners and forwarded to their homes . . . all being grateful for what had been done for them.'

The Skerries have a long reach. In November 1966 it stretched to the coast of the Isle of Man.

The 1,287-ton Greek freighter *Nafsiporos* had emptied her holds in Liverpool and she was carrying very little ballast when a cyclone hit her as she crossed the Mersey Bar. Her young skipper Angelo Katsovufis—at 28 the *Nafsiporos* was his first command—decided after discussions with the first mate Evangelos Pittas, only a year older than himself, to run for Ramsey Head where he could ride out the storm under the shelter of the cliffs.

Somehow they managed to make the haven through terrifying seas. Then, on December 2, with no sign of the storm abating, the *Nafsiporos* began to drag her

An aerial picture of the 'Nafsiporos' in the moments before the Moelfre and Holyhead lifeboats made their first rescue runs.

Daily Express.

anchor. Soon they were drifting crabwise on a wild sea driven by a gale which was gusting at 100 m.p.h. Chief Engineer John Patsoulas came on the bridge to report the screws were being lifted clean out of the sea and with no resistance to slow them were turning at so great a speed the engines were overheating.

He warned: 'It's only a matter of time before they break down altogether.'

The first radio warning of the *Nafsiporos's* danger was logged at 8.20 a.m. when she was reported twelve miles south of Douglas Bay. The Douglas lifeboat, the 46-ft *R. A. Colby Cobbin No. 1*, was launched but, with visibility at 500 yards, her coxwain Richard Lee had little hope of finding her. She was drifting quickly now. At 9.50 a.m. the Ramsey coastguard reported she had drifted 11½ miles. An hour later a Shackleton from RAF Kinloss found her 25 miles off Douglas Head. Coxswain Lee estimated he was within five and a half miles of the new position but though he searched all day he could not find the *Nafsiporos*. At 6.30 p.m., her fuel dangerously low, the *Cobbin* had to return to her station.

Meanwhile the freighter, minute by minute, hour by leaden hour, was drifting onto the rocky jaws of the Skerries.

On Anglesey that morning the Holyhead RNLI secretary, the late Tudor Roberts, had been warned that the *Nafsiporos* had been sighted out of control 20 miles off Point Lynas. He tried to 'phone Tom Alcock, a former bowman on the Rhyl lifeboat who had just been appointed coxswain of the Holyhead station but all phone lines had been blown down. Anxiously Roberts ran out of the house, the storm pulling at his coat tails, to round up a crew as best he could.

He had hardly left before Lt. Commander Harold Harvey, the RNLI Inspector of Lifeboats, arrived to make a courtesy call. On hearing the news he too set off for the boathouse where he arrived to find consternation—there were no phones working, the maroons could not be heard over the gale, there was no time left for a physical

'Nafsiporos' adrift, December 1966.

Daily Express.

search and therefore no way of collecting a crew. Harvey offered his services as an extra hand and at 10.30 the *St Cybi*, a 52-ft Barnett class lifeboat, was launched into a north-westerly gale, Force 10, gusting to Force 11.

For three hours in appalling weather the *St Cybi* searched until at 1.30 p.m. they sighted the Shackleton. Radio contact was made and the aircraft was able to guide the *St Cybi* to the *Nafsiporos*.

Help was now reaching the Greek ship from all quarters. A Russian timber ship, the *Kungurley*, had picked up her May Day and after many attempts had been able to get a tow aboard although by now the *Nafsiporos* was yawing 60 degrees port and starboard and most of her crew had been injured as they rolled around the deck like marbles.

The tow only held for 25 minutes before it snapped under the pressure of a beam sea and once again the *Nafsiporos* was sent skittering across the wave tops.

The Moelfre lifeboat, the *Watkin Williams*, had been out since 7.40 a.m. and her crew were glad when they approached the slipway in heavy seas just after 1 p.m. Within the hour they would be sitting down to hot meals before blazing fires. They were half-way up the slip when the winchman, Richard Lewis, shouted urgently for the coxswain, Richard Evans, to take a phone call from the Holyhead coastguard. It was a call to go to the aid of the *Nafsiporos*.

Cold, tired and still desperately hungry, cox and crew waited, shivering, while the *Watkin* was refuelled. At 1.55 p.m. they launched again, against the wind and into an ebbing tide.

Like the *St Cybi*, the *Watkin Williams* was carrying a senior ranking officer as an extra hand. Captain David Jeavons had been master of six Canadian Pacific Steamship Company vessels ranging in tonnage from 3,500 to 27,000 tons. He had been at his home in Moelfre when the maroons had gone up, on leave before taking com-

The Moelfre lifeboat the 'Watkin Williams' during trials after repairs in the Menai Straits. RNLI.

mand of the *Empress of England*. At once he ran down to the slipway to volunteer for a jacket.

Later he was to tell an RNLI inquiry:

'The sea and weather on December 2 was certainly not what deep sea men would regard as boating weather. To call conditions extreme is really an understatement and I was truly impressed by the strength of the lifeboat.'

The seas were daunting even to veteran lifeboatmen like Evans, his second cox Murley Francis, his son David, crewmen Hugh Owen and Hugh Jones, Evan Owen the mechanic and his deputy William Maynard Davies. When the rescue was over Evans told reporters: 'They were like nothing I'd ever been told about. We climbed perpendicularly and we went down the same way. I was afraid every wave was going to send us somersaulting on our backs.'

The waves were not Evans's only worry. An RNLI coxswain knows his own patrol area as well as his own back garden, in some cases better. He carries his charts in his head and every hazard is engraved on his mind. But the *Nafsiporos* was lying outside the Moelfre patrol area. Evans and his crew were in waters of which they knew nothing, the compass was veering madly and visibility was now practically nil. If they opened the cabin door to get to the charts the sea would come flooding in and a very short time after they launched the radio was wrecked by a wave that hit them like a fist. With winds gusting on the starboard bow at 120 m.p.h. and through 32-ft waves the Moelfre men had to find the *Nafsiporos* by dead reckoning, a feat of prime seamanship.

So great was the force of the seas the *Watkin Williams* met that the deck ventilators were ripped away and green water flooded the bow under the foredeck. Murley and David Evans, putting their lives at greater hazard with every step they took, had to scramble forward to stuff the holes with spare life-jackets.

Wrestling with the wheel, Evans could only watch his son and his best friend and pray . . .

When the *St Cybi* sighted the *Nafsiporos* she was making no way at all. A helicopter from RAF Valley which had by this time joined the rescue made a gallant attempt to winch a man down to her deck but the wind tossed the helicopter aside like a paper glider.

Alcock brought the *St Cybi* round the *Nafsiporos's* stern only to be met by a great wave running down her side which lifted his lifeboat high above the freighter's deck and then dropped her into its trough behind with her screws churning like circular saws only feet above the lifeboatmen's heads.

A ship's boat which the crew had tried to board swung on a single davit spinning madly, dangerously near the jumping ladder. If it struck the lifeboat when she went alongside it would sink her. But they had barely time to assess the danger before a second wave smashed the *St Cybi* against the iron hull of the freighter making her timbers rattle like loose teeth.

The *Watkin Williams* came on the scene just as the *St Cybi* was making her first run and when yet another giant wave sent the *St Cybi* sheering away in its spume Evans decided to make his first approach. Calculating the speed of the tide which was ebbing strongly east to west, setting against it the speed of the lifeboat, he brought the *Watkin* in a wide arc and came in from the west. Twice he repeated the manoeuvre, his crew gesticulating to the Greeks to jump. But they would not budge.

Alcock watching realised the terrified crew would have to be snatched from the *Nafsiporos* in the few moments when either lifeboat could come alongside. Although the *Nafsiporos's* anchor had at last bitten into the sea bed she was now lying in only five fathoms of water less than a quarter of a mile west of the East

103

Mouse rock. Lashed by 100 m.p.h. gales, battered by waves 35 feet high, she was yawing violently 35 degrees either side of the vertical. It was work which required a highly skilled bowman but the *St Cybi's* regular man was not in the crew. Only Alcock, for several years bowman of the Rhyl boat, had the necessary skills.

With little time to make a decision Alcock called Harvey to take over the helm while he scrambled up the foredeck with his second cox, William Jones.

Harvey, quickly getting the feel of the boat, positioned the *St Cybi* to the tide using engines and rudder and laying down to hit the *Nafsiporos's* beam on at the foot of the jumping ladder. Fortunately in the moment of impact a wave lifted them, pitching and rolling twenty feet up the freighter's side and, like small boys scrumping apples, Alcock and Jones plucked off five seamen and threw them into the *St Cybi* before she fell with the dying wave.

A shout from Harvey followed by a shuddering impact froze the two men to the deck. The dangling ship's boat had parted from its single davit and crashed on the deck where a moment earlier they had been standing. The lifeboat's radio mast buckled under the impact and a pair of oars whistled through the windows of the wheelhouse missing Harvey by inches. Fortunately the *St Cybi's* movement sternway and a fortuitous wave combined to carry the wreckage overboard ripping the guard rails as she went.

Once again it was the turn of the *Watkin Williams*. A beam wave which hit her as she came alongside smashed her against the freighter—but somehow Evans managed to keep her steady in line with the jumping ladder long enough for Francis and David Evans to grab ten more crewmen.

'New boy' David Jeavons was filled with admiration. He said later: 'The men on the deck on the port side of both lifeboats took terrible risks. The *Nafsiporos* and the lifeboats were roaring towards each other which meant that the men on the port side

The 'Nafsiporos' 2.12.66.

Daily Mail.

risked being totally crushed. The Greek seamen were reluctant to leave and had to be literally dragged off the side. This meant that the men on deck were on the port side for a long period of time taking extreme personal risks. Personally I was amidships catching the bodies as they were thrown across and was not in much danger. I was therefore able to observe the risks the other men were taking. One other thing: the engineers were absolutely terrific. The remarkable response from the engine rooms—instructions had to be shouted over the noise of the wind and sea—undoubtedly saved disaster on that day.'

In the end, the sea did not claim the *Nafsiporos*. Her young skipper and four of the crew elected to remain aboard, her single anchor held and in time she was towed by the tug *Utrecht* through the rocks to safety. The next day when the storm abated she was towed to Liverpool and a month later the lifeboatmen received their awards.

The RNLI awarded gold medals, its highest honour, to Commander Harvey and Coxswain Evans; silver medals went to Coxswain Alcock and to the mechanics of the two boats, Eric Jones of the *St Cybi* and Evan Owen of the *Watkin Williams*. To every other member of both crews went bronze medals for their part in what has been recognised as one of the most dangerous and difficult services in the history of the RNLI.

Pirates and Gun-runners of Holyhead

Stealthily, like a sea thief, the Clyde steamer *Fingal,* her speed well below her 13 knot maximum, edged round the breakwater at Holyhead. The three-day voyage from Greenoch had been made in a full gale and the crew were exhausted.

The date was October 15, 1861. Across the ocean on the Potomac River the American Confederate Army were short of every kind of ammunition and the *Fingal's* holds were crammed with military supplies. She had been bought by Confederate agents and loaded by night. She carried 14,000 Enfield rifles with bayonets, 500 revolvers, two 4½-inch breech loaders, a large quantity of ammunition, gunpowder and medical supplies destined for the Confederate Army which was defending Richmond, Virginia.

Secrecy was essential. Yankee lobbyists had initiated the British Proclamation of Neutrality which forbade the transportation of contraband of war and the American Consul in Holyhead was ever alert to news of Confederate gun-runners.

In hiding in Holyhead were the Confederate arms buyer, Colonel Edward Anderson, a Liverpool ex-merchant seamen John Low who had joined the Southern cause and James D. Bulloch, a Southerner, who, when the Civil War broke out, had been commanding a US mail steamer.

A man of scrupulous honour he had insisted on returning the mail steamer to her owners in New York before escaping through the Northern enemy lines to join the Confederate Navy which at that time consisted of one ship. More were needed to resist the inevitable blockade by the North and, since there were no shipyards in the South, Bulloch was sent secretly to Liverpool to buy ships with a budget of millions of dollars. Posing as the agent of a private shipping line he had arrived on June 4,

1861, and within a month the keel of the first foreign built Confederate cruiser, the *Florida,* had been laid in the yards of William C. Miller and Sons. Although she was built using the basic design of a Royal Navy gunboat, shipyard workers were told she was destined for a Palermo merchantman. A little later work started at Lairds on a second warship, the 220-ft long barque-rigged *Alabama.*

Both ships would sail out of Liverpool as merchantmen. It was while he was waiting delivery of the two vessels that Bulloch, dodging the detective the US government had employed to watch him, slipped away to Scotland to buy the *Fingal.* Now he waited anxiously in Holyhead for news of her safe arrival.

She was almost round the breakwater when out of the mist loomed the masts of a brig, the *Siccardi,* an Austrian vessel at anchor with a full cargo of coal. A hoarse cry of alarm from the watch, the clang of a bell, a jolt that shook the munitions in the hold and the whine of engines being thrown into reverse. Too late. The sharp prow of the *Fingal* sliced into the brig's starboard quarter. There was a sound like the snap of a gun-hammer, then a shout from the deck of the *Siccardi.* But before a boat could be lowered the brig sank like a stone under the weight of her cargo of coal, every man aboard drowned, victims of a war that was being fought a world away.

Day was just breaking when Bulloch was wakened with the news of the sinking. Pulling on clothes as they ran to the quay, Bulloch, Anderson and a Texan doctor called Holland tumbled into a punt and rowed out to the scene of the wreck. In the half-light they could make out the upper spars standing straight up out of the water, the bunt of the ship's main top gallant just awash.

Bulloch knew there was not a moment to lose. Customs officers would already be on their way. For a certainty they would board the *Fingal* and that would be the end of her days as a Confederate gun-runner. The US Consul in Holyhead was already suspicious of her and he would use every legal device he could summon. At best the *Fingal* would be delayed by a string of affidavits.

Bulloch thought of the rifles and munitions in the hold and of the ill-armed pickets on the Potomac who needed them so desperately. In a moment he had made up his mind. He wrote a hasty letter to his Liverpool broker authorising the payment of compensation to the *Siccardi's* owner. Then he ordered the skipper to weigh anchor and the *Fingal* had cleared the point of the breakwater and was steaming down channel before anyone in authority had realised there had been a collision.

Nor was luck to desert him for the rest of the voyage. The only problem Bulloch had failed to solve was finding a secret rendezvous where the ships now being built in Liverpool could be fitted out as men-of-war. Running out of water in the Azores he put in by chance at the village of Praya on the north-eastern coast of the island of Tenceria. It was the perfect anchorage for a rendezvous. And, despite running aground in the Savannah Estuary, he went on to deliver his cargo of guns.

Sadly when Bulloch left the *Fingal* he took his luck with him. Renamed the *Atlanta* and fitted out as an armoured gunship with four 7-inch cannon, the vessel ran aground and struck her colours during her first engagement with two US Navy monitor ships.

Bulloch meanwhile had returned to Holyhead, crossing the channel in heavy storms in the single-engine steamer *Annie Childs*. It is unlikely he paid much attention to the weather. He was busily engaged in plans for getting the other two vessels, the *Florida* and the *Alabama,* out of the Mersey.

The *Florida* proved no problem. She reached Nassau without incident on 13 May, 1862, and on her first voyage destroyed 14 US ships and took ransom notes from four more. She continued to harry shipping for two years until she was captured by a stratagem in the neutral port of Bahia, Brazil.

The *Alabama* was launched two days after the *Florida* docked in Nassau. Clearly, although no one in the shipyard knew she was to be a man-of-war, it was going to be difficult to get her out of the Mersey. The US authorities had broken Bulloch's cover and events began to move swiftly. On land American diplomats lobbied the British government to seize the *Alabama* and the US ship of the line *Tuscora* put off from Gibraltar to search her out and sink her. Bulloch had to move quickly.

On Saturday, May 26, 1862, he asked Lairds to fit the ship out for an immediate sea trial. To allay the surprise of US agents he invited a party of Liverpool dignitaries to come aboard the *Alabama*—at this time commissioned under a Spanish name, the *Enrica*—to enjoy a day at sea while she went through her paces. The US agents were completely taken in. They watched the *Alabama,* dressed in gay bunting, sail down the river. And if they did notice a steam tug, the *Hercules,* following in her wake they probably thought no more than that it was a sensible precaution.

Bulloch was the most affable of hosts and when at 3 p.m. he announced he was going to keep the *Alabama* out that night to complete her trials no one was the least concerned. After all, as he pointed out, the sea was quite smooth.

'We will run close to the Bar and everyone can go back in the tug,' he explained. To the captain of the *Alabama* he issued secret orders to anchor off Moelfre to await his return.

Back in Liverpool he courteously bowed his guests off the tug. At 7 a.m. the next morning he received news that the *Tuscora* was steaming north to intercept the *Alabama.* He set sail and by 4 p.m. was alongside the Conferate ship. At 1 a.m. the next morning he set sail in a south-westerly gale. He was just in time. The next morning the *Tuscora* sailed into the bay. At Terceira the *Alabama* was armed with

110

six 32-pounders, one 8-inch smooth bore, one 7-inch 100-pounder, two 11-inch guns pivoted on the deck and a 28-pounder pivoted on the top gallant forecastle and a 12-pound howitzer. With this formidable armament she spent the next two years almost constantly at sea until she was sunk in the Battle of Cherbourg by the US ship *Kearsage.*

Meanwhile in Liverpool Bulloch won much sympathy. The news that his new ship had sunk with all hands was believed by everyone . . .

. . . except perhaps the US Consul.

Bulloch also bought two paddle steamers in Holyhead from the London and North Western Railway Co., who at that time ran the ferry service from Anglesey to Ireland.

Few shipping lines can have had worse luck with their vessels than the LNWR.

On April 17, 1863, their paddle steamer *Telegraph* ran aground near South Stack. On September 8, 1875, two of their ships, the *Edith* and the *Duchess of Sutherland,* collided at the end of Holyhead breakwater. A month later the LNWR paddle steamer *Earl Spencer* collided with a Llanelli steamer, the *Merlin,* which sank near the breakwater. On October 31, 1883, the company's steamer *Holyhead* struck a German barque and both were sunk. On January 4, 1887, the paddle steamer *Banshee* ran aground at Porth Tywyn and the steamer *Eleanor* which was sent to tow her off grounded on the same bank. A year later almost to the day *Earl Spencer* was in trouble again when she went aground on rocks beyond Holyhead break-water. In 1900 it was the *Eleanor's* turn again. She rammed another of the company's vessels, the *Connemara,* which in turn, on March 20, 1910, rammed and sank a cargo steamer off the Skerries. For the *Connemara* it really was a case of third time unlucky. On November 3, 1916, she was rammed and sunk by a collier.

In the light of this unhappy record the Admiralty's decision to requisition four LNWR steamers on the outbreak of World War I verges on the foolhardy. It was unwise to ignore the jinx. The first ship, as *HMS Tara*, was torpedoed a year later in the Mediterranean, the second struck a mine in the Straits of Dover in the same year, the third was sunk by a torpedo and the fourth by a mine in 1917.

By general consent the jinx was operating at its most malevolent aboard the *HMS Tara* which had been the *Hibernia* when she sailed with the LNWR.

When war broke out the *Tara* was fitted with two ancient Hotchkiss six-pounders mounted forward with a third one aft and despatched to patrol the North Channel between Scotland and Ireland. During the next year she set up a Royal Navy record by steaming 60,000 miles in those treacherous waters before returning to Holyhead for a refit.

Her next posting was to Alexandria where she became part of the North Egyptian Coastal Patrol making a daily call at the port of Sollum where a tiny British force of one hundred was surrounded by thousands of cut-throat Senoussi tribesmen. When the *Tara* was torpedoed the 92 survivors were picked up by a U-boat but the commander refused to land them near the English garrison at Sollum. Instead he took them to Port Bardia which was in enemy hands.

From there the crew, many of them 'railway sailors' from Holyhead, some in their 60's and 70's, who had been requisitioned with their ship, were force-marched for hundreds of miles under a sadistic Egyptian through the Red Desert of Libya. When they reached their prison camp, a small and squalid oasis, they were guarded by Senoussi who alternately flogged and starved them until finally they were rescued by the Duke of Westminster leading a squadron of armoured Rolls Royces he had bought himself and fitted out for war.

The greatest wartime tragedy to an Anglesey crew happened on October 10, 1918.

The German High Command, realising the war was lost, had made the first overtures for an honourable peace treaty with the Allies. But there were still U-boat commanders hunting the narrow channel between Holyhead and Eire who were interested neither in peace nor in honour. While Prince Max, the Kaiser's son, sued for peace a new submarine campaign was being mounted. New, more heavily armoured U-boats slid from their pens to sink the troop ships which were bringing American soldiers into the war.

The *SS Leinster* was not a troop carrier. Owned by the City of Dublin Steam Packet Company the twinscrew vessel had been the pride of the company's line since her commissioning in 1897. A 3,000-tonner, her 9,000 h.p. engines were capable of a top speed of 24 knots and she made the 57-mile passage between Kingstown and Holyhead twice daily in 2 hours, 45 minutes.

From neutral sources directors of the line had been warned repeatedly that the *Leinster* was a target but, unaccountably, the Ministry of Shipping ignored repeated requests from them for a naval escort. When she sailed out of Kingstown on her last voyage with 687 passengers and a crew of 70 she was alone and defenceless.

She was twelve miles out of harbour on a beautiful morning, clear with a bright sun, when the first torpedo hit her, ripping off her bows and causing dreadful carnage. Just aft of the bows was the GPO office where twenty-two men worked sorting the mail. Only two escaped alive, one blown by a freak blast through the hole the torpedo had made and the other scrambling over twisted metal to the deck.

A survivor who was on the second deck just above the sorting office described the scene:

'When the explosion occured every light went out. Water came rushing in and I felt the ship plunging and sinking fast down by the head. In the dim light I saw flames rushing up from the Post Office room and smelled a strong sulphurous smell. The little ladder leading down to the sorting office was broken and I could hear men shouting in the darkness. Water was flooding in and only one man, dripping wet, managed to climb out.'

The master, Captain Birch, had been hideously disfigured when the explosion smashed the glass windows of the bridge into his face. Yet with one eye literally hanging out on his cheek he still retained control. When the smoke cleared he put the mail steamer about to run for the Irish coast. If the watertight compartments held he had a fighting chance, but as a precaution he ordered the ship's boats to be lowered. The first boat was swinging on its davits, filled with civilian passengers, when the U-boat commander loosed his second torpedo. The result of this sadistic act was devastating. The torpedo struck the *Leinster* midships in the engine room.

John Jones of Holyhead, the fourth engineer, was one of the few members of the engine room staff to survive. Back home in Orton Road he remembered how he had been in the stokehold when the first torpedo struck. He ordered the firemen out and began an inspection of the engines. But something made him follow the other men. He had just left the stokehold when the second torpedo struck.

Said Jones; 'There was a terrific explosion and the ship seemed to split from stem to stern.'

Hugh Jones, the second steward, had been in the saloon pantry when the first torpedo struck and had rushed forward to help lower boats:

'We got one down but before we could lower the second we were struck amidships and I was thrown into the water.'

An anonymous survivor painted a graphic picture of the next moments when he returned to Holyhead.

He said: 'But for the second torpedo the water tight compartments would have kept us afloat until help arrived. As it was boats were being got out from the davits.
114

A couple had been floated and were picking up those people who had jumped or been thrown into the sea. There was a rope over the side near me. I waited until a lifeboat came under it then I slid down the rope and flung myself into it. There were at least thirty already there, including two or three women.

'The second torpedo struck the ship not far from our boat. It was the most awful spectacle I have ever witnessed; it happened in clear view of the boats.'

The *Leinster* was listing to port and nearly down by the gunwales at the forepart; the stern was high in the air, the propellers clear out of the water, when the second torpedo struck. There was a terrific explosion followed by the splintering of decks. Plating, spars, coal, cinders, boats and rafts were all blown into the air on a black cloud. Boats and rafts in the water were lifted by the blast and smashed into driftwood. Everything was scattered in the great black cloud burning oil and debris. Her funnel, boilers and engine rooms were blown to pieces. One moment she was a damaged but still seaworthy Royal Mail steamer, the next she had ceased to exist. Nothing was left but odds and ends of wreckage. The *Leinster* was not so much sunk as blown away. One man recalled that she literally crumbled into ashes.

Some of the boats which got away, already dangerously overcrowded, shipped seas and sank leaving their occupants struggling in the heavy swell.

The first rescue ships, Royal Navy destroyers, arrived within an hour and a quarter and sailors hardened by four years of war were sickened by what they saw. Most of the ship's boats had been sunk in the explosion and scores of bodies floated like broken dolls on the swell.

Captain Bitch, despite his injuries, had survived the second explosion and had managed to swim to one of the few boats where another survivor, J. H. Cropper, a Liverpool man saw him:

'We were crowded and there was no room on the boat for him. But he was obviously in very great pain and eventually we lifted him half into the boat with his legs dangling in the water. When we were picked up it was very difficult to get from our lifeboat to the destroyer. We had to jump at the precise moment the waves lifted us level with the decks and hope the sailors caught us. I fell twice before I made it. Before I was taken below I saw the captain still hanging half in and half out of the water. I never saw him again and I assume he was washed away to his death.'

Meanwhile every available craft had put out from Kingstown and a fleet of 20 ambulances lined the wharves and streets leading to the docks. None went away empty. Two hours after the sinking the first survivors, a stoker smoking a cigarette with careful nonchalance, stepped ashore from a rescue ship to be mobbed by the waiting crowd.

The *Leinster* was the fifth cross-channel packet to be lost in the war including the *Connemara* which went down with all hands. But she achieved something that none of the others had managed. The next mail steamer which left Holyhead a day later had a destroyer escort.

Since Roman times when she was the last fortified outpost on the Empire's western flank Holyhead has suffered from every kind of naval aggression.

In 1631 the robbers who attacked the mail packets were Arab corsairs, in 1649 Irish Loyalists. In 1656 the Puritan Military Governor, Major Thomas Swift, had to watch powerless with his garrison while Irish pirates boarded and captured two of his ships and after seizing everything else stripped the clothing from the crew and sent the captains ashore to raise a £50 ransom for their ships.

Such audacity did not always bring success. A vessel flying English colours arrived off Holyhead in the 18th century firing cannons as a distress signal. In fact she was a French privateer and when customs men went to her aid they were seized and held to ransom. But that night the privateer hit bad weather. Dismasted and out of control she was driven onto the rocks at Penmon Point. Once again her cannon boomed out a distress signal but, fearing it was another trick, the rescue boats stayed in port until daybreak. The privateers—over one hundred in number—ended their adventure in Beaumaris Gaol.

Their ship's guns were silent for the next 112 years until August 1822 when they were used to fire a Royal Salute to welcome George IV to Holyhead.

In World War II the port was once again under enemy attack. On 22 July, 1940, *HMS Campina,* a 290-ton trawler, called up for patrol duties struck a mine and sank just beyond the New Harbour lighthouse. A month later the 1,598-ton cargo boat *Lady Meath* sank after hitting a mine at the breakwater. On that occasion the patrol boat *Manx Lad* also struck a mine when she went to her aid. In April 1941 the inn which Major Swift, the Royalist Governor, had built was destroyed by a German bomb.

Lifeboat Lady and Charter Gold

In the century and a half since it was established the Holyhead Lifeboat Station has saved over 1,500 lives. The waters it patrols are commonly agreed by mariners to be some of the most dangerous off Britain and but for the determination of a 19th century parson's wife the toll of life would certainly have been greater.

Frances Lloyd, a Caernarvon girl, had been fascinated by the sea since childhood. While her sisters sewed she employed herself drawing the first practical chart of the Menai Straits and when she married the Reverend John Williams she was in her element. Williams's parish was Llanfairynghornwy on the Anglesey coast. They were not long back from their honeymoon when they witnessed a drama at sea which was to alter the course of their lives.

On March 26, 1823, the packet boat *Alert* was in passage from Dublin to Liverpool. At 10 a.m. when she was some distance to the east of the Skerries the wind dropped, the seas fell calm and with a strong ebb tide making to the west the crew were alarmed to find that their ship was being driven onto the West Mouse rock. A boat was hurriedly hoisted out under the command of the mate to tow the *Alert* out of danger by the brute strength of its rowers. Since the *Alert* was carrying above one hundred passengers it is not surprising the attempt failed and the *Alert* struck the skirts of the rocks as she drifted past, ripping a great gash in her side.

As water poured inboard, overwhelming the hand pumps, the ship's officers put passengers to work baling water in buckets from the hold and passing it by human chain up to the deck and over the side. Other passengers, lost in panic, refused to take part in the salvage and jumped over the side, some to their deaths on the rocks. A few managed to reach the ship's boat which took them aboard until it was so full it almost sank.

118

The captain, clearly not a man who believed in going down with his ship, pushed his way through the terrified passengers running aimlessly about the deck, scrambled to the bowsprit end and jumped into the sea. Although the ship's boat was full, the mate threw his skipper a rope and the captain, five crew members, a cabin passenger and five deck passengers were towed ashore like fishing net floats.

Once his passengers were safely ashore the mate and three of the crew put out to sea again rowing through the breakers to the wreck. They found three more passengers using two crates of eggs to support themselves and they were saved. But the local boatmen who joined them lifted twenty-nine corpses out of the sea and when the final count was made the captain and all his crew, except a steward and a boy, were saved but one hundred passengers perished.

To the Reverend Williams and his wife watching helplessly from the shore the lesson of the *Alert* was obvious. Though well-intentioned the efforts of the local boatmen were unco-ordinated and too late. They had only learned of the disaster when the first survivors came ashore. From this realisation was born the idea of an organised rescue service with sea watchers to give the alarm at the first signs of a ship in distress.

From those small beginnings the Anglesey Lifeboat Association was born. Frances Williams set out to raise funds to buy a boat by selling sketches, bullying the gentry for subscriptions. She worked tirelessly and it was not long before the first craft was put on station at Cemlyn Bay.

Nor was her husband idle. He became cox of the boat and took part in every service on which she was ordered. Ironically he made his most famous rescue without her.

On March 7, 1835, the *Active* out of Belfast was wrecked in the bay and began to break up in breakers so high that it was impossible to launch the boat. Nothing daunted, the Reverend Williams who had galloped up at the first warning put his horse at the sea and swam it out near enough to the *Active* for him to throw a grappling line into her bowsprit rigging. As a result of this brave action the crew of five were saved and the Rev. Williams was awarded the first RNLI Gold Medal—the Lifeboatman's VC—to come to Wales.

By the time the Anglesey Association was taken over by the RNLI in 1856, by feats like this, the Williams rescue service had saved over 400 lives.

The Cemlyn boat saved all the passengers and crew when, due to a pilot's error, the 1,130-ton iron steamer *Olinda* was wrecked on the Harry Furlongs reef on 26 January, 1854. Built only nine months earlier at a cost of £35,000 the *Olinda* was outward bound for South America with a £50,000 cargo. After she struck the reef the force of the tide turned her completely about so that she was holed on both sides.

Another outward bounder the SS *Arctic* ran aground at Point Lynas on March 18 the same year. Although she was able to get back to the Mersey shipyards under her own steam her life at sea was to be a short one. On September 27 that year she was rammed by the French steamer *Vesta* in thick fog off Cape Race. When news of the loss of 351 of her passengers reached New York the city was draped in mourning cloths.

Not all the ships that were damaged on that coast were the victims of its tides.

The flat boat *Wellington* lost its rudder in Amlwch Harbour on January 28, 1817, as a direct result of a bad harvest. The wet summer of the previous year and the sparse harvest which resulted brought hardship throughout Wales. Hill farmers in Merioneth and Mongomeryshire starved; in Cardiganshire the peasants lived on boiled nettles and on Anglesey the price of bread was so high that few of the men who worked in the copper mines on Parys Mountain could afford to buy it.

The near slavery of the mines, the appalling conditions under which the men had

Wreck of the auxiliary steamer 'Olinda' near Cemlyn, Anglesey.

Gwynedd Archives Service.

to work and the pitifully low wages they received had produced in Amlwch a bitter and resentful population. Fear of an approaching famine stirred rebellion and when it was learned that local farmers and contractors planned to export all their grain to more lucrative markets in Liverpool passions rose still higher. A group of workers rowed out to the *Wellington* which was loaded with oats and oatmeal, removed her tiller and hid it in the churchyard.

For several days angry mobs roved through the streets and on February 3 two magistrates arrived to swear in thirty special constables. They had difficulty in finding anyone to take the job. One magistrate complained that no sooner were constables sworn in that 'they considered their duty done and disappeared except five or six who were totally inactive with the exception of one'.

The first attempt to recover the tiller failed. The magistrates did arrest the ringleader of the men who had hidden it but they had trouble taking him to Beaumaris Gaol. On the way they were attacked by a mob and had to bundle their prisoner into a post-chaise.

Thoroughly roused, the mob stoned the magistrates at every attempt they made to move the ship. A paper threatening the lives of two mine agents was posted on a smithy door and an informer disclosed a plan to storm Beaumaris Gaol. Finally, a hundred and sixty four of the 45th Regiment were brought over from Dublin to look for the tiller but it was only after three days of riot patrols that the *Wellington* was made ready for sea. Even then it was four days more before she sailed and only then after local landowners agreed to raise £400 to finance harbour improvements and road repairs.

Few wrecks have been more written about than that of the *Royal Charter*. Charles Dickens was the first of a troop of authors to be seized by the drama of the disaster. So vividly did it etch itself on the public mind that, although 135 ships were sunk, 90 damaged and 800 lives lost, the storm which caused the havoc is still known as the *Royal Charter* gale.

There had never been a hurricane like it in this country. The first shipping it caught when it blew up on Tuesday, October 25, 1859, was the Channel Fleet, at excise off the Eddystone. Gusts of over 100 m.p.h. scattered the vessels and tore up coastal embankments and railway lines in Devon and Cornwall.

'Royal Charter' : artist unknown.

The gale hit Anglesey at 8 p.m. Outside Holyhead Harbour the much publicised iron paddle steamer *Great Eastern* all but sank at her moorings while inside wooden ships were smashed into sticks. The next day ships dragged at their anchors to be pounded against rocks; at Flint a factory was levelled to the ground. At Liverpool Observatory a wind force of 28 lbs to the square foot, the highest ever, was recorded and the sea level rose by four feet.

And into this holocaust of wind sailed the *Royal Charter*. She was a lovely, graceful craft; a 2,719-ton clipper built expressly for the Australia run at Sandycroft boatyard on the River Dee below Chester. By the standards of the day she was the last word in luxury. She had a sick bay and even a laundry, just rows of washing tubs but even so a facility available on few ships of the day.

Her maiden voyage had been a disaster—she sank a short distance from the boatyard—but she was to become the pride of the Australian Steam Navigation Company's fleet. Her first run to Australia had been a dazzling triumph. Just under 60 days after leaving Plymouth she anchored off Melbourne and her owners advertised:

'The Magnificent Steam Clipper *Royal Charter*. Australia in under sixty days.'

Her passengers on the return trip to Wales were mainly successful miners bringing home the riches they had made in the Australian gold fields. When the *Royal Charter* sailed from Melbourne with a crew of 103 and 324 passengers she was carrying besides her cargo of wool and sheepskins an estimated £500,000 of gold in her strong room.

The passengers were delighted with the *Charter*. When she reached the Irish coast in record time a testimonial was subscribed for the captain, Thomas Taylor. In the general atmosphere of jubilation lady passengers made up another purse for the Rev. Charles Vere Hodge, a passenger who had conducted services during the two-month run from Australia.

124

The passage to Holyhead was enlivened by the prospect of seeing the *Great Eastern*, that wonder of the age which its designer I. K. Brunel had brought for sea trials off the Anglesey coast. They had hoped to persuade the captain to change course so that they could have a sight of this 700-ft long, 20,000-ton iron monster which, it was claimed, would take 3,600 passengers. But the captain, mindful of his vessel's reputation for speed and, no doubt, the company's advertising slogan, refused to change course. He felt confident that he could improve on his time outward bound. The weather had been fine during the entire voyage, the wind now was from the south-east, light and favourable, and he was in sight of Liverpool. He looked forward with justified optimism to the congratulations of his owners. Then at 8 p.m. the glass fell and the wind changed. Soon a heavy gale blew up from the east, whipping up fierce squalls that tore at the rigging. As they passed the Skerries under a darkening sky the first white crests broke on the heads of the heavy swell.

The *Royal Charter* had been signalling for a pilot since 6.30 p.m. and at 7 p.m. the signal was picked up by Richard Parry on Pilot Boat II. But within an hour he was fighting for his own life in a 100 m.p.h. hurricane, his pilot boat pinned like a brooch on the bosom of waves that reared as high as houses. It was impossible to reach the *Charter*.

By that time, pitching and rolling heavily, for not even her 200 h.p. engines could hold her steady, the *Royal Charter* was making hardly any way at all. She was carrying fore and aft sails and a single top gallant but at 8.30 with the wind pushing them beam on across waves like mountain ranges towards the rocks at Point Lynas Captain Taylor ordered the topsail set and told the helmsman Owen Williams to starboard the wheel. By this manoeuvre he hoped to bring the *Charter's* bow into the wind and thus reduce her resistance, but she was no longer responding to her rudder. Taylor ordered soundings to be taken. The first call was '18 fathoms' but the second minutes later was '15': his ship was drifting leeward onto the rocks.

At 10 p.m. Taylor ordered the 100-fathom port anchor paid out and an hour later the starboard anchor. Together they brought the *Royal Charter* temporarily to a halt but after little more than two hours the port cable snapped just short of the hawser hole. There was a stern anchor in the chain locker and Taylor ordered it brought forward. It took a seaman an hour to find it, drag it along the deck and mount it. It had hardly been paid out before the starboard anchor cable snapped.

At 3 a.m. in four fathoms of water the *Royal Charter's* keel scraped the bottom and she struck. She was soon stuck fast. Her bow canted and she was brought high and upright on a stony beach, broadside on to the sea and only twenty yards from the rocky shore. To the passengers it seemed a miraculous deliverance. The plateau of rocks was so near that in the deceptive half-light it seemed that a man with a walking stick might touch it. They waited, their fears gone, to see what ingenious method the sailors would use to get them ashore. Many of the miners no doubt saw themselves back in their local inn surrounded by admirers whilst they told exaggerated stories of shipwreck. In the saloon the Rev. Hodge held an impromptu service of thanksgiving for deliverance while on the deck the captain and his officers moved among the passengers with reassuring words.

'The ship is quite fast and low. When the tide goes out we will be able to walk ashore,' Taylor told them.

He may even have believed it himself.

The lifeboat station at Moelfre is only a quarter of a mile from the rocks where the *Royal Charter* struck and rockets were sent up, guns fired according to the manual. But the captain must have realised quite early that no pulling and sailing lifeboat could hope to live in such a sea. Ordering all the passengers below, he signalled for the masts to be cut away. They fell like the forest trees they had once been, their progress slowed by the tangled rigging they brought down with them. The sound as they crashed onto the decks must have terrified the passengers below but at least they were spared the sight which gripped at the hearts of the crew. In half-light the waves had seemed high but in the full light of early morning the crew watched petrified as roller after roller, sixty feet high, pounded the ship.

Twenty-five yards away was the shore. At the top of the cliff, so near that every detail of their features was sharply etched, the villagers of Moelfre stood in stunned, silent groups watching the drama which was being played out below them. So near land yet the *Royal Charter* could not have been in greater danger if she had been anchored in the eye of the hurricane.

At the peril of their own necks villagers scrambled down the cliff to meet Joseph Rodgers, a seaman who had tied a rope round his waist and jumping over the side had swum to the shore. Willing hands dragged him onto the rocks, untied the rope and used it to draw a 10½-inch manila hawser from the *Charter* to the land where it was lashed to a rocky outcrop. A makeshift bosun's chair was rigged and preparations made to evacuate the ship. Incredibly, although the hurricane was worsening, many of the lady passengers refused to use the chair on the grounds that it was immodest.

Sixteen people were brought ashore but it was slow work against the pitching and rolling of the *Royal Charter* and the long wait began to tell on the passengers. As they realised their danger their apprehension grew—until by 5 a.m. it had exploded into panic. Some despairing of ever reaching their turn on the chair jumped into the sea hoping that they would be thrown ashore on a wave crest; others tied themselves to spars and then jumped. Some were saved, but most of the 450 men, women and children who died that morning were lost in that mad half-hour of panic.

The first jagged rent appeared in the side of the *Royal Charter* at 7.30 a.m. and the

A contemporary artist's impression of the wreck of the 'Royal Charter' near Moelfre in 1859.

sea reached through it to drag out its victims. Some time later, as the *Charter* yawed, the hawser which carried the bosun's chair tautened and snapped—and three men who were on it, and only a few yards from safety, fell to their deaths.

The wreck of the 'Royal Charter' off Moelfre in 1859.

The shore by now looked like a seascape in hell. Sheepskins, clothing, rolls of hide and luggage bobbed and spun in the surf. The mutilated bodies of the dead lay in heaps where the sea had tossed them. and in rocky crevices, in small islands of sand, tumbled in piles by the sea, glistered the bright glint of gold. The products of hard years of mining lay unwanted now next to the bodies of dead owners.

The fate of this fortune in gold has been argued over ever since. Fortunes were made that night by plunderers of the dead but the gold lust was not confined to simple islanders. One aristocratic landowner tried to get a court ruling that, since the wreck occurred on his estate, all the gold was his! He lost his case.

From the first the Establishment showed more enthusiasm in guarding the gold than it did in the succour of survivors or even the removal of the dead. A company of Royal Marines from *HMS Hastings* was sent to Moelfre as soon as the underwriters learned of the disaster. Aided by coastguards, policemen and a detachment of the English Militia they sealed off the area of the wreck while twenty villagers were put to collecting the gold. Sadly, the Marines seem to have fallen below the usual high standard expected of that distinguished corps. When a Margaret Morris refused to leave the beach a Marine grabbed her. She lashed him in the face with a wet sheepskin, the watching crowd began to cheer and then to stone the Marines who broke and fled. They were chased all the way back to Moelfre and two local men took advantage of what was literally a shining opportunity and collected £900 in gold!

One story of plunder, possibly apochryphal, will serve for all.

A coast watcher, Dan Williams, is said to have seen his neighbours Will and Jenny Jones collecting gold on the beach. In turn Will was watching the watcher and warned his wife who immediately stuffed £40 worth of gold they had collected down her bodice. Leaving her husband she made her way home where she put the gold in a saucepan, covered it with winkles and put the pan on the fire. She was innocently laying the table when Williams, the coast watcher, arrived and insisted on searching the house. He found nothing but when he had finished he was so tired he was glad of the plate of winkles Jenny offered him from the pan.

Whatever the truth of that story, certainly fortunes were made. The *North Wales Chronicle* reporter on the spot recorded:

'. . . there were many robberies perpetrated on the wreck. Yesterday we were shown some bills of exchange, printed in red ink, and drawn on the Union Bank of Australia which had been taken from a drunken man on the coach from Amlwch to Menai Bridge.'

The *Daily Telegraph* went so far as to demand the death penalty for the plunderers. In rebuttal the angry villagers published a list of the names of 28 who had risked their lives to save the survivors. But even today stories of the *Royal Charter* gold and the families it enriched can produce a stormy reaction in Moelfre.

A Chapter of Coincidences

Exactly one hundred years and a day after the *Royal Charter* disaster a second sea drama was played out in exactly similar weather conditions within half a mile of the clipper's grave. And one of the heroes of the second drama was a descendant of Richard Matthews, the Moelfre villager who gave the first alarm and led the rescue attempt on the night the *Charter* struck.

When Coxswain Richard Evans, MBE, was admitted in 1978 to the Gorsedd of Bards at the National Eisteddfod at Cardiff—the highest honour his country could pay him—he was given the Bardic name 'Arwr y Don' ('Hero of the Waves'). It is an apt description of Britain's most decorated living lifeboatman, the holder of two RNLI gold medals.

Medals are not rare on the Moelfre station. Men from there have been awarded four RNLI 'golds', 26 'silvers', 29 'bronze', five Queen's Silver Medals for Bravery at Sea, 15 Humane Society medals and one BEM. Of these 'Dick' Evans, as he is known all over Britain, holds two of the gold, the BEM, one of the Queen's silver medals and a bronze medal. He has also been awarded the RNLI 'Thanks on vellum' and the Maud Smith award for saving life at sea. He is an Honorary Fellow of Manchester Polytechnic and in 1967 after he appeared on a moving 'This Is Your Life' programme he was voted one of Britain's 'Men of the Year'.

Nowadays Dick lives in retirement at Moelfre, fishing, tending his small boats and lecturing all over Britain raising funds for the RNLI.

As his biographer it has been the present writer's good fortune to hear the stories of all the rescues in which he has taken part during his 49 years service with the RNLI. Since he joined as a boy of 16 the Moelfre boat has been launched 179 times

The Moelfre crew gather to wish Dick 'God speed' in his retirement.

and 281 lives have been saved: but of these rescues none, I believe, more perfectly demonstrates the courage of Britain's lifeboatmen than the epic rescue of the crew of the *MV Hindlea*, a 506-tonner out of Cardiff in ballast from Manchester to Newport.

On 26 October, 1959, while Dick and his crew were attending the memorial service which is held every year for the dead of the *Royal Charter* at Llangallo church (where many of them are buried) the *Hindlea* was fighting for her life in similar conditions in the same patch of sea in which the *Charter* was lost.

Early next day, in a relief lifeboat, the *Edmund and Mary Robinson*, a craft of which he had only taken delivery the previous day and which he had been warned was a difficult boat to handle, Dick and a crew of four—one of them a novice making his first sea trip—braved some of the worst recorded seas to go her aid.

There are no better words to relate this epic of the sea than Dick's own—as he sits on his boat on the beach at Moelfre, pipe glowing and looking twenty years younger than his 74 years.

'You see, every lifeboat I have been coxswain of belonged to me. The RNLI had nothing at all to do with it. It was my lifeboat, I thought the world of it. Even a scratch on the paint was like a scratch on my own body. It was my whole life.

'But I knew very little about the *Edmund and Mary Robinson*, the relief boat. She was totally different from my lifeboat, the *Watkin Williams*. She was a modern lifeboat with modern means of navigation. There was nothing like that in the *Edmund and Mary Robinson*. She was an old boat, in fact 26 years of age, and I dreaded thinking of going out in her until I had what we seamen call the 'feel' of her. How would she take a beam sea? How would she run before a gale? Every boat takes the sea different. Some lifeboats can run before any sea. Others can't.

134

The 'Edmund and Mary Robinson' reserve lifeboat used in the rescue of the 'Hindlea'.

'Little did I think of the experience I was to have with this boat.'

Dick was helping his wife to prepare lunch on October 27, 1959, when the testing time came.

'I received a telephone call from the coastguard, Captain Owen Roberts, that a ship was dragging her anchor in Lligwy Bay. The wind was rapidly veering to the north and she was being driven towards the rocks. All the other ships had managed to get out to sea but the *Hindlea* was riding hard.

'I immediately went down to the boathouse. By this time the wind was blowing a full hurricane from the north, ninety miles an hour and still increasing. Slates were being blown from houses and I had to dodge from being hit. Hay from the small-holdings had been torn from the stacks and was hanging from the telegraph wires. I could hardly stand.

'The mechanic, Evan Owen, was already at the boathouse and the lifeboat engines were running. Also my second cox, Murley Francis, had gone to the boathouse thinking that we were bound to be needed. Another member of the crew, Hugh Owen, arrived. Now we were four. I could not telephone the remainder of the crew, all the phone wires were blown down.

'The coastguard, Captain Roberts, came to the boathouse. He was frantic. He asked me to launch the lifeboat immediately. I very well remember his words. He said, "I hate having to send you boys out in this terrible storm. But that ship is being driven onto the rocks and once she gets into the breakers you won't get near her."

'There was one man in the boathouse, Hugh Jones, who helped on the slipway. I asked him would he volunteer and he immediately responded—although he had never been in a lifeboat before.

'If these four men would have refused nobody could have blamed them. It was almost suicide to go out in a lifeboat in such terrible seas. But as soon as I said "We'll go boys" they immediately climbed the ladder into the lifeboat. I instructed them to make sure their life-jackets were tied down and we fastened each other's to be sure—although I'm afraid they would have been of little use in that terrible sea. By now the wind was gusting up to 104 m.p.h. A northerly wind is the worst possible wind in Moelfre Bay. It was *Royal Charter* weather.

'I'd never been out in the *Edmund and Mary Robinson* in bad weather but we cleared the slipway and the crew hauled the radio masts up. I told them to pack themselves under the forrard canopy. I had to tie myself to the wheel. It isn't an easy thing to do. The sea was a boiling mass of fury. My grandfather taught me all the seamanship he knew but he never taught me how to deal with this kind of sea. It was coming up from all angles.

'The *Hindlea* was only about half a mile from the slipway but it took us an hour and a half to get to her. The sea in the bay was terrible. What it would be like on the other side of Moelfre Island I had no idea. I did what I always did in the lifeboat. I prayed. I prayed desperately. There were only four words in the prayer and I must have said them continuously, "Please God Guide Me", and I'm sure I would not be talking to you today unless some superhuman power had guided me that day.

'This is something not clearly understood by any of us but I am absolutely certain that every time I prayed I felt a renewed strength running through my body.

'The *Hindlea* was about one and a half miles north of Moelfre Island. Her anchor was still dragging. She only had one anchor down. She should have had two but the captain could not send his men to the fo'c's'le head to put the other anchor down. They would have been washed overboard. She had this one anchor out with 100 fathom of chain and she was striking rapidly. She had got into real trouble. She was veering to 90 degrees with the engines racing. I decided to go up on the lee side but by the time I approached her she was yawing so much I was coming up on her weather side.

'When she was about 200 yards from the rocks the master gave orders to abandon ship and the crew of eight lined up on the port side of the deck. Huge seas washed clean over her. I looked at my gallant crew and, believe me, they were gallant men. I knew them well, I knew their families. I'd nursed their children. I thought to myself "What right have I to take these men to their deaths?" A coxswain has to make terrible, cruel decisions and this was surely one of them. I knew they trusted me and their lives were in my hands. But I could hear a faint cry "Save us, lifeboat" and I knew we had to try.

'Now the ship was in the breakers which I had been afraid of all the time. I decided to come about, and just before I turned the boat round I thought of my own wife and three sons, probably sitting by the fire, huddled together, listening to the wind howling and the rain lashing against the window: waiting for the telephone to ring and afraid of answering it. But there was no time for sentiment. Eight men were going to die soon unless I did something. I came about and edged the lifeboat round the stern of the *Hindlea*. When you run against a breaking sea you usually put a drogue out to keep the stern of the boat dead on the breakers but I couldn't use a drogue. We were so near the rocks it could easily have tangled with the propeller and that would have been the end of us all. I had to run in through the breakers without it. It was a tremendous strain on my arms—turning the wheel to keep her head on to the sea.

'I intended to come in on the port quarter. As we passed her stern the *Hindlea's* propellers were whining above our heads and we were just round when we were hit by a solid wall of water. It was the biggest wave I have ever seen in my life. It was like a mountain. It could have swamped us and the *Hindlea*. The little lifeboat rolled right over on her beam ends, her mast going under water. Desperately I fought to bring the lifeboat under control. I thought it was the end: she was capsizing. I used

138

maximum engine revs to stem the sea, then, slowly at first, at an angle of 25 degrees to the coaster, she came up like a fighting cock.

'Now the two boats were thrown violently against each other. I could see the propeller. It was three yards from tip to tip and whirling round like a windmill. It was only 15 feet away and it would have cut us into chips if we'd drifted under it. I knew now that the lifeboat was going to be seriously damaged—but she still responded to the helm and one man jumped from the *Hindlea* into the lifeboat.

'Hugh Owen, an old friend, dashed out from the canopy, ignoring seas that could have washed him away for ever. He dragged him to shelter. Instantly we were washed 30 yards away from the ship. We had to go back. In fact we went back ten times in all. As the lifeboat was lifted on a wave, level with the *Hindlea's* deck, one after the other her crew jumped into my boat until there was only one man left.

'By this time the *Hindlea* was terribly close to the rocks. Now I had another terrible decision to make. Would it be wiser to leave that one man and save the men who were already in the lifeboat? Yet: I knew I could not leave him behind. I took a desperate gamble and drove the lifeboat back again to the *Hindlea* where the man was hanging from the side.

'Suddenly I felt the lifeboat being lifted up the side of the ship and before I knew where we were she was sitting high and dry on the deck of the *Hindlea*. We just had time to grab the last man before a second wave lifted us clear.

'Now we were in real trouble, trying to get out of these terrible breaking seas. The *Hindlea* was very, very close to the rocks; the wind was screaming as we came clear. I had to put the boat beam on to the sea to get round Moelfre Island. I knew that my crew were not in good fettle and the survivors were in a very bad way. Time was of the essence. I nursed the *Edmund and Mary* like a child, bringing her head on to the breaking seas and then, when I saw a lull, edging her round. I could not see the

The rescue is over. Ten lives have been saved and the effort it cost is written in every line on Dick's face. The photograph was taken after the 'Nafsiporos' rescue.   Radio Times

island for the seas breaking over it. I had to turn the boat now and run before this terrible sea without the help of a drogue. There were 13 of us in the boat, the crew and survivors jammed together under the canopy, me at the wheel.

'My waist was sore from the chafing of the ropes I had used to lash myself to the wheel and my hands were too numb to unfasten the knots. If we had capsized I'd have had to go down. Every so often I had to hammer my fists against the wheel to get the circulation going. My eyes were sore and gummed up with salt. In the end a single wave at least 30 feet high swept us on its crest the whole length of the island and we found ourselves alongside the slipway.

'As they had done down the centuries the women of Moelfre were waiting to take the survivors to the chapel vestry where there was a roaring fire, dry clothes and hot food. I sat on the slip utterly exhausted. My eyes were caked up with salt, my cheeks were bleeding and I was desperately tired. Suddenly I realised tears were streaming down my face.'

When Dick Evans reported the rescue to his Head Office he was ordered not to take the lifeboat out again until she had been completely overhauled. But within 25 minutes he was at sea again, going to the aid of a coaster with a flooded engine room.

'We got a rope onto the ship and waited for a call to take the crew off. We were desperately tired. We had been out since mid-morning and now it was evening. But we knew the Beaumaris lifeboat had been ordered to launch and relieve us. They had a terrible passage coming from Beaumaris Sound into a northerly hurricane. They took over at 6.30 p.m. and we returned to Moelfre. We got the boat onto the slipway. By now the crew were exhausted and I sent them home. I went with Evan Owen, the mechanic, to his house where his wife made us a meal. Then we went back to the boathouse and spent the whole night trying to patch up the damage to the lifeboat.

141

Mrs Owen brought us tea and coffee to keep us awake and then, at 6 a.m., I had a call to relieve the Beaumaris lads. I fired the maroon and to my amazement the same gallant lads who had been on the *Hindlea* service were the first to arrive.

'Lifeboatmen have tremendous guts. You've got to know them to know the sort of men they are.

'Out we went to stand by the coaster. It was still a very rough sea but it was moderating. About 11 a.m. a tug boat arrived from Liverpool. We followed them until they were round Point Lynas. It was 3 p.m. when we pulled up the slipway.'

Hugh Owen, who was a veteran member of the lifeboat crew which went to the *Hindlea*, had been a boy in an earlier epic rescue by the Moelfre boat. The lifeboat was called out on October 28, 1927, when the ketch *Excel* carrying a cargo of coal from Birkenhead to Holyhead got into difficulties off Carmel Head.

When she started to ship water her skipper, Captain John Ballance, decided to run for Moelfre. His engine room was flooded and the bulwarks were disappearing one by one. Then the main gaff came crashing down on the deck and the ketch was completely out of control. There was nothing now that Ballance could do but wait for the lifeboat.

A young man, Tom Williams, who was making his maiden voyage in the lifeboat left an impression of the service.

'We were a long time finding the *Excel*. In fact we were told on the way it was hopeless to look for her and were advised to return. But we couldn't do that. We carried on. It was blowing a full gale and the seas were very bad.

'When we did sight the *Excel* she was almost awash. A German freighter was trying to take her in tow and her crew of three were signalling us to take them off. That decided us; but we weren't sure how we were going to get alongside in such a sea. Waves were piling over the *Excel* and she looked like foundering any minute. We

142

headed for her midships hoping that a wave would carry us aboard. By great good luck we managed it. We drove at her on the crest of a big wave; our bows grounded on the deck of the vessel and crashed into a hatch. No sooner had we touched her than the three men in her crew scrambled aboard and in less time than you could count ten our stern had dropped and we slipped off again. I never saw three men more delighted.'

Their joy was premature. The lifeboat had sprung a leak and sustained heavy damage when it hit the deck of the *Excel*. Darkness fell and the gale grew wilder. The lifeboat's lanterns were washed overboard; it would be hopeless to attempt to return to Moelfre. All the crew could do was to hold tight to their lifelines while the lifeboat beat about, waiting for the dawn. Most of the time they were under water. Williams sat most of the night up to his chest in water, nursing the 66-year-old veteran of the crew, Will Roberts, who had been injured when the boat crashed on the ketch's deck. Despite the youngster's efforts a particularly large wave pulled Roberts from his arms and washed him overboard. Williams and another man, John Owen, lifted him back but the shock had been too great and he died shortly afterwards.

Said Williams: 'It was impossible to keep your seat. Someone or other was always tumbled off by the sea and bruises and cuts were freely received. Our worst trouble was brine in the eyes. I closed my eyes once and when I re-opened them I could not see. Salt had dried over them and when I tried to brush it off it went into my eyes.

'At about 1.30 in the morning we made Puffin Island but the wind and tide were against us and it was impossible to reach the shore. All we could do was cling to our lines and wait for morning. It was then that Will died. His last words were a request for a chew of tobacco.'

The 500-ton coaster 'Hindlea' breaking up on the rocks near Moelfre in 1959 at almost the same point where the 'Royal Charter' had foundered a hundred years earlier.   Daily Mirror.

Some time later that night a second man died, Henry McGuinness, a member of the crew of the *Excel*.

The Beaumaris boat had been launched, when a motorist arrived from Moelfre with the news that the station had lost contact with their boat. The Beaumaris cox searched all night from the north of Point Lynas, then, at 5.30 a.m., he saw distress signals from the direction of the Lavan Sands. At last the adventure was over.

In Moelfre the *Excel's* captain paid a moving tribute to his rescuers. He said:

'The weather was fit to kill anybody but they stuck to their guns. The lifeboat was waterlogged and she was as often under the water as she was on top of it. There could never have been a better crew. The man at the tiller stood bareheaded—his sou'wester had been blown away—from 3 p.m. on Friday until 7 a.m. on Saturday with his hands on the tiller and when he arrived at Beaumaris his eyes were almost closed as a result of the salt. It was just as though his eyes had been plastered over with sand.'

The 'man at the tiller' was William Roberts, the uncle of Dick Evans of the *Hindlea* and the great-nephew of Richard Matthews of the *Royal Charter*.

Rescue Projector erected ready for firing. Rescue Rocket inserted and connected to 250 fathoms of 1 inch nylon rocket line.

146

1

Firing a rescue rocket projector showing the stages. Neilson Photographs. **3**

2

'Dive . . . Dive . . . Dive . . .'

The weather was fine and from the deck of the submarine the crew could see every spar in the dockyard cranes which stretched along the Mersey bank like the skeletons of dinosaurs.

A sullen, grey bludgeon when she had lain in the dock at Birkenhead, the submarine was transformed when the crew cast off and she moved like one of her own torpedoes down the estuary to the sea. Below decks with the hatch down the memory of the clean salt air above stayed with the crew. The submarine was crowded for her first sea trials and already the air inside her smelled like the barrel of an old sporting gun. Usually the full complement of submarines was fifty six but on this day there were one hundred and three men on board. Besides her crew there were civilian technicians, a Mersey pilot, shipyard fitters to make last minute adjustments and observers from the Admiralty.

Frank Shaw, a 31-year-old charge-hand fitter from Cammel Lairds, was happy enough. This was the submarine he had worked on and it was a pleasant change to get away from the dockyard clamour for a day. He listened intently to the main propelling machinery as he stood, spanner in hand, by the auxiliary motor outside the engine room.

When Lt. Commander G. H. Bolus had done his rounds he stood under the periscope watching the Admiralty senior observer Captain H. P. K. Oram filling in the first of the sheaf of forms he carried, bulldog clipped to a Bristol board. Bolus was nervous. Although the responsibility for the submarines was his the captain outranked him and was besides an experienced submariner. If Bolus made a mistake Oram would notice. But there was nothing he could do. He signalled to the steward

148

and while the sub bucked in the considerable surface swell, all hands were given bottled beer and meat pies.

Captain Oram nodded to the steward to put his victuals down when they arrived and filled in first the date of the trials. '1st June, 1939', and then the name of the submarine: '. . . HMS *Thetis*'.

Oram knew about submarines, he had watched them building his own first submarine, *HMS Regulus*. He had already made a mental note of one irregularity. It was not usual, he knew, to carry so many men on these trials. Normally everyone except those hands needed to operate the diving machinery was taken off by a tug before the submarine submerged. But he reflected these were not normal trials. Despite reassuring reports from Munich by the Prime Minister, Neville Chamberlain, service chiefs were hurrying their preparations for war and many necessary short cuts were being taken. In happier times the *Thetis* would never do her first diving trials at sea, he reflected. The established practice was for them to be carried out in the comparatively safe waters of the Gaerloch. Bolus would need to use extra caution in the dangerous waters of Liverpool Bay.

On the attendant tug, *Grebecock*, ploughing in the wake of the sub, the R.N. Liaison Officer, Lt. Richard E. Coltart, went through the details of the drill he had worked out with Commander Bolus. Before she dived the *Thetis* would hoist a red flag above her periscope so that he could follow her progress by tracking it through the waves. Neither man seems to have appreciated that the small flag would be almost indistinguishable when it was soaked in sea water.

In the event of a mishap a system of signalling by explosive charges had been arranged. A code was worked out for tapping messages through the hull and a buoy with a telephone attached would be released by the *Thetis*. In fact there was no telephone on the buoy, but, as he braced himself on the deckhouse, Lt. Coltart was confident that all precautions had been taken.

Nine miles off the Great Ormes Head at 1.45 p.m. the *Thetis* made her first dive. Coltart knew at once that something was wrong; after looking so light on the surface the sub became heavy too quickly in the dive.

Inside the *Thetis* the crew had taken up diving stations three quarters of an hour before Bolus gave the order to dive. At 1.40 p.m. the commander signalled his intentions to the Fort Blockhouse at Plymouth. At this stage all but the men concerned with the mechanics of the dive would have been transferred to the tug. The reason they were not was never discovered but when the *Thetis* went down on her first and only dive she took all 103 aboard with her.

Her torpedo officer, Lt. Frederick Woods, was a conscientious man. When the crew had gone to diving stations he toured the tube and torpedo compartments and the crew's space, then he made his way amidships to the control room where Chapman, the first lieutenant, handed him the 'trim chits' which would tell him how much water the torpedo tubes and the auxiliary and compensating tanks contained.

Against numbers five and six torpedo tubes he read 'full'. Satisfied the ship was stabilised, Lt. Woods went back to his own diving station in the torpedo compartment where he ordered a vacuum test throughout the sub. Satisfied there were no leaks he made his report and braced himself for the dive. It was slower than he thought it should be and he decided to check the torpedo tubes to see if they really were full as the chits had indicated.

When he opened the test cocks only a trickle of water came from number six tube and number five tube was completely dry. He made his way back to the control room where Chapman told him that the tubes should have been full. Robinson, the foreman engineer at Cammel Lairds, disagreed.

Noticing that the trim of the submarine had been adjusted by filling the compensating 'A' storage tank, Woods suggested he should fill the torpedo tube to assist the dive. Chapman agreed and Woods returned to the torpedo room.

The bow caps on the outer rims of the tubes were controlled on the *Thetis* by manually operated levers on the bulkhead. Open they would bring the sea rushing in. Woods saw that both bow cap indicators read shut. It was safe and he began his final, fatal inspection.

When he came to number five tube he found the rear door lever was stiff and it was some time before he could get it open. Finally it began to move. A second later the door was flung back and a torrent of water crashed into the torpedo compartment. A dock yard painter had neglected to rime the test cock in the rear door. It was blocked by bitumastic enamel in the closed position. Although Woods had no way of knowing it, the outer bow cap which kept the submarine watertight was open.

Suspecting none of this he assumed the tube was fractured and struggled to close the rear door against the torrent of water which was pouring in. Despite his efforts the tube compartment was flooding fast. Woods shouted to his deputy, Chief Petty Officer Mitchell, to signal the commander to blow the main ballast tanks.

In the control room Oram was giving the same advice to Bolus but it was already too late. The *Thetis* lurched and began to settle nose down, the stern lifting above the wave. She had sunk in a depth of water only half her own length.

Mitchell waded through the flooded compartment to Woods' side and together they tried to bring down the clips which would hold the door. It was impossible to move them at the crazy angle in which the sub was lying and Woods ordered the evacuation of the torpedo compartment. The lights had failed by this time and he found himself struggling for the after door in pitch darkness against an avalanche of tables, stools and boxes which had been flung across the cabin by the motion of the sub.

Bolus ordered a smoke candle to be fired and the forward indicator buoy released. And then occurred the first of what the Inquiry Judge, Sir Alfred Bucknill, called 'the persistent ill fortunes' of the rescue operation. The buoy had no telephone and in any case was not seen by the *Grebecock*.

Lt. Coltart, of whom Sir Alfred observed 'he found it difficult to decide upon the proper course of conduct when the *Thetis* disappeared', was later to offer an explanation of conduct which it is difficult at this distance of time to understand.

He said: 'Three quarters of an hour after she dived the *Thetis* would have been about four miles along her course. It would have been very difficult to see her periscope at that distance. The red flag would have been very wet and would not have shown very well, although one might have seen it. It was a fine day with good visibility.

'I gave orders to up-anchor at 4.15 p.m. to 4.30 p.m. I was trying to get a signal through Seaforth to Fort Blockhouse reporting her disappearance and that I was anchored in her last known position. But the radio telephone was very weak. While we were trying to get through I heard from the Blockhouse that the duration of the *Thetis* dive was three hours from 1.40 p.m. Therefore at 4.40 p.m. I gave up trying to send the signals because I knew she was overdue and further action would be taken from the Blockhouse.'

The rescue operation was delayed, according to the inquiry report, because the rescue vessels were misled by the anchored position (some miles away from the sub) of the *Grebecock* and a report from an aircraft of a buoy which proved to be miles away from the position of the wreck. It was not until 7.30 the next morning that

HMS Brazen saw the *Thetis*'s stern sticking out of the sea and sent down explosive charges to signal that rescue was at hand.

Meanwhile on the sub, his pockets filled with metal bolts as ballast and carrying an ordinary torch he had made waterproof by sealing it with electrician's insulation tape, Lt. Chapman, the first officer, tried to get through the escape hatch. But the escape chamber was flooded and Chapman stumbled back into the control room wracked with pain, his lungs and ears bursting.

Woods and Mitchell made the next attempt. When they climbed into the chamber Woods looped a rope round his chest while Mitchell lashed the end to a bulkhead plate. Woods planned to swim to the torpedo chamber and he arranged a code of tugs on the rope for Mitchell who would be paying out the rope behind him.

Gradually the chamber filled with water until it was level with their eyes. The pain was agonising. Woods managed to relieve it by holding his nose but Mitchell could not get his hand to his face and this second attempt had also to be abandoned. Once again Woods tried but when this too failed Bolus ordered that no more attempts should be made. It is a tragic irony that none of them realised that the escape hatch was only 15 feet below the surface of the sea.

At 7 p.m. every man aboard could have reached the surface through the escape hatch. There was still a large reserve of air in the pressure tanks but the officers decided against using the Davis apparatus. They believed, not unreasonably, that in the heavy swell the men would drown. It was decided to wait for outside help. Tragically the rescuers outside were waiting too—for the men to escape through the Davis hatch.

The next morning at 6 o'clock Woods woke from a shallow doze to find breathing difficult. He had a headache, but some of the older men aboard were obviously in worse distress. A rating was trying to close down a set of valves but he was having

The salvage operation of 'H.M.S. Thetis'. She lay in water shallower than her own length.

Daily Mirror.

154

difficulty in co-ordinating his movements and Woods took over from him. Most people were lying down now although it was difficult on the sharp gradient of the deck. He saw Bolus signalling him. He went to the control room and found all the other officers. After Bolus had outlined their situation he asked for two volunteers to escape through the Davis hatch. Their chance of survival was believed to be so slight that messages telling the state of the sub would be strapped to their legs in case they were dead when they were picked up.

Oram and Woods volunteered and slowly, painfully, began to crawl up the deck, by that time sloping at an angle of 42 degrees. Although the hatch was only a few feet away it took them a quarter of an hour slipping on the film of oil which covered the iron deck plates and being passed along from man to man to reach it.

Their first attempt to flood failed but as the chamber was being drained for a second attempt the men inside heard their first message of hope. From outside came the dull explosion of the charges sent down by *HMS Brazen*. Moments later Oram and Woods had surfaced and were picked up by a whaler from the *Brazen*.

In the submarine conditions began to deteriorate rapidly. Frank Shaw, the fitter, had his first hint of the disaster when he had felt a sudden rush of air coming aft. The sub took on a list, there was a bump and the *Thetis* began to plunge, throwing him against the watertight door of 69 bulkhead. Conditions worsened through the night; by the morning men were vomiting and groaning all round him. Water had seeped into the electric storage batteries and the chlorine gas produced was swirling through the ship.

The drill for escaping through a Davis hatch was basically simple. Two men wearing breathing apparatus entered the hatch through a door at the bottom. The chamber was flooded to form an air lock and when the internal and external pressures had equalised the outer hatch was opened and the men passed to the surface in the bubble formed by the air lock. In theory two men could be sent to the surface every five minutes. In fact the operation is not quite so simple as it appears, training and a degree of mental agility are needed to operate the mechanism. Weakened by chlorine and their night under water the men were tired and clumsy. Tragically the escape was delayed when four men tried to get into the chamber at the same time. One after another they died of heart failure and valuable time was lost draining the hatch and removing the bodies. Shaw who was teamed for the escape with a stoker named Arnold watched as the men were lifted out.

'One was still just alive. I asked him why they did not get out and he said, "We couldn't open the hatch." '

The sight of the dead men and fear that the hatch might be jammed were not the best incentives for going into the chamber. But the alternative, to die slowly and painfully of chlorine gas poisoning, was too terrible to contemplate. Shaw stepped into the chamber behind Arnold. He recalled:

'Stoker Arnold helped me to put on my escape gear and we stepped into the chamber together. It began to flood and just before the water came up to our mouths we put on our mouth pieces. Stoker Arnold told me to try to lift the hatch. It would not go. I tried twice and it did not go, the pressure in the chamber had not equalised. As soon as it did the hatch opened easily and we shot to the surface in a few seconds.'

They were the last men to leave the *Thetis* alive.

Even today the reasons for the delay in mounting the rescue operation remain unclear. The Inquiry ruled out lack of vigilance by the responsible staffs ashore.

Sir Alfred offered three suggestions at the Inquiry:

'It was due partly to the absence of any reason to suppose that such a strange accident would happen; partly to a desire not to cause unnecessary alarm and partly to a

156

'Thetis'.

reluctance to set a number of ships and men in motion as required by the procedures laid down if it proved to be a false alarm.'

They do not, it must be said, appear compelling reasons and one wonders what submariners thought in 1940 when they read Sir Alfred's comments as they prepared for sea.

Whatever the reasons, it was 3 a.m., nearly twelve hours after the *Thetis* had disappeared on a dive of a three hours maximum duration, before the rescue ship *Vigilant* embarked from Liverpool. There were further delays due to misinformation and the *Vigilant* did not reach the *Thetis* until after the *Brazen* had arrived.

Once it was begun, the rescue operation quickly gained momentum. Two submarines, the *Cachalot* and the *Porpoise* which carried powerful air compressors, were despatched to the scene. Three divers were flown down from Scapa Flow where they had been clearing the scuttled World War I German fleet. They landed at Speke where a lorry was waiting to take them to a destroyer, *HMS Matabele,* which was awaiting them in Liverpool Docks.

At 12.55 on the morning of June 3 the first diver Sinclair McKenzie put on his equipment, a waterproof inflatable suit, ungainly boots heavily weighted with iron and a huge spherical iron helmet. He made the first dive in a five-knot tide and had to fight for his life every inch of the way down, hanging on to the drag rope with both hands to prevent himself being swept away. At last he reached the sea bed. It was pitch dark and, with no electric gadgetry to aid him, he had to walk along the sea bottom with outstretched arms until he bumped into the metal hull of the *Thetis.* He took a 4-lb hammer from his belt and tapped reassurance on the hull.

He waited and then, faintly, from inside the *Thetis* he heard answering taps.

He said later: 'It was quite impossible to tap out any morse signals at that depth. I was down to the extreme limit of my air pipe which was 300 ft long. I was working at

'Thetis'.

Daily Mirror.

an acute angle and in danger of being swept away. The tide was increasing in strength and I knew that I would be lucky to get back to the surface. If I had let go of the drag rope or the pilot rope which quickens our ascent I would have been lost. I had to go up. It was terrible. I had to come up hand over hand, hanging on to the rope. By the time I took off my helmet I was exhausted.'

McKenzie surfaced so quickly he had to be sent down to the 30-ft mark to be decompressed to rid his blood of the nitrogen bubbles which might otherwise have killed him. But the time he spent at the *Thetis* was not wasted. He had memorised every inch of the skin of the sub he had touched and from this underwater braille he was able to give salvage experts a precise drawing of the position in which she was lying. But it was too late. Because of the unusually strong tides and the shallow depth at which the *Thetis* was lying the divers could only work for half an hour on either side of high tide.

Said one diver: 'We knew we were working on a coffin.'

Meanwhile efforts were being made to cut a way into the *Thetis* through her stern. But the rowing boats from which the cutters worked bobbed about on the swell and the *Thetis* rocked and pivotted in the under-current. It was impossible to hold the torches steady to cut through first the outer skin, then a watertight door and finally, in the confined space between the two metal skins, cut through a second watertight door into the sub.

After 50 hours the rescue operation ceased. Now it was merely a question of salvage.

In contrast to the rescue the salvage operation was a brilliant piece of improvisation. Cables were dropped from the rescue boats *Vigilant* and *Salvo* while three tugs, *Storm Cock, Holm Cock* and *Crosby,* anchored close by. On the bottom at 26 fathoms the divers passed the cables under the *Thetis* and brought them back up to the surface so that the *Thetis* rested on giant slings. No machinery existed at that time strong enough to lift the 2,000-ton sub. Instead, the engineers harnessed the power of the sea lifting her 11 ft on each rising tide and shortening the slings accordingly. After the tides had lifted her to the surface the tugs towed her to Anglesey where she was beached in Lligwy Bay. The bodies of the 99 dead were brought ashore and taken to Moelfre lifeboat station for the macabre work of identification.

A veteran lifeboatman who saw them described the scene quite simply as 'the worst moment of my life.'

'Thetis'.

Daily Mirror.

The submarine 'Thetis' beached at Moelfre.   Gwynedd Archives Service.

On April 5, 1940, the 62-page report of the Inquiry was published. In it Sir Alfred listed the factors which he said had produced the disaster.

1.   The complete blocking of the test cock in the rear door of No. 5 torpedo tube with bitumastic enamel.

2.   The opening of the rear door at a time when the bow cap of the tube was open to the sea. The precise moment it was opened was critical and the most obscure point in the case.

3.   The failure of those on board the *Thetis* to close effectively the port water-tight door in the bulkhead between the torpedo tube compartment and the torpedo stowage compartment.

4.   The failure of those in the *Thetis* to expel the water from the two flooded compartments.

5.   The failure of those on board to escape through the apparatus.

On the *Thetis* is was not enough to be dead. You had to take the blame as well.

Summing up Sir Alfred said: 'A series of mishaps delayed and misdirected the search on June 1 and it was not until 2 June that she was found, just as the four survivors were surfacing. Believing that others were on their way rescue operations were suspended.'

He added: 'If those in charge of the salvage operations from the time the stern came into view had concentrated their efforts on holding it up out of the water and getting oxy-acetalyne gear as quickly as possible to cut a hole in the stern more men might have been saved.

'The danger of cutting such a hole was that if the ship's stern lost its buoyancy and sank beneath the surface the steerage compartment would be flooded . . . The reason why this method of escape was not used was that those in charge of the salvage at first expected the majority of those on board to escape through the hatch.'

No one, it seems, saw fit to ask why the brilliant improvisation of the slings was not used to rescue the men, only when all hope was gone the submarine.

It may be that the currents were too strong under water to tap out a morse message on the submerged hull but it surely would have been possible to tap out such a message of intentions on the stern which was well above the waves.

When all the bodies had been removed the *Thetis* was towed back up the Mersey to be refitted. A year later, re-named the *Thunderbolt*, she sailed again. None of the crew knew that they were serving on a death ship and for three years under her skipper Lt. Commander Bernard Crouch DSO and Bar she harried the enemy, sinking two U-boats and five enemy supply ships. In 1943 she vanished.

This time there were no survivors.

Bibliography

The Secret Service of the Confederate States in Europe by James D. Bulloch (1883)
Royal Yachts (London 1932) by C. M. Gavin
The Drums of the Birkenhead by D. Bevan
Prisoners of the Red Desert by R. S. G. Watkin Williams
Transactions of the Anglesey Historical Society
Shipwrecks of North Wales by Ivor Wynne Jones
An account of the Wreck of the Royal Charter by E. Nell Baynes
Wreck and Rescue on the Coast of Wales by Henry Parry
Britain's Lifeboats by A. J. Dawson
The Golden Wreck by Alexander McKee
Memoirs of Sir Llewellyn Turner, 1859-70, ed. by J. C. Vincent, 1903
Tacitus
Sir William Bulkeley's Diary
Pepys Diaries
Evelyn's Diary
The Lifeboats of Cardigan Bay and Anglesey by Henry Parry
The Uncommercial Traveller by Charles Dickens
Anglesey and North Wales Coast Pilot by Henry Glazebrook
Across the Straits by Kyffin Williams
Maritime Wales — Gwynedd Archives
Narrative of the loss of the Rothesay Castle in Beaumaris Bay by R. J. Morrison, (Lt. R.N.)
Files of the Liverpool Daily Post; the North Wales Chronicle; the News Chronicle and the Daily Dispatch

Index